Veil

Veil:
Mirror of
Identity

CHRISTIAN JOPPKE

polity

First published in 2009 by Polity Press

Reprinted in 2010 (twice)

Polity Press
65 Bridge Street
Cambridge CB2 1UR, UK.

Polity Press
350 Main Street
Malden, MA 02148, USA

ISBN-13: 978-0-7456-4351-9
ISBN-13: 978-0-7456-4352-6(pb)

A catalogue record for this book is available from the British Library.

Typeset in 11 on 13 pt Scala
by SNP Best-set Typesetter Ltd., Hong Kong
Printed and bound in the United States by Odyssey Press Inc.,
Gonic, New Hampshire

For further information on Polity, visit our website: www.politybooks.com

Pour Catherine, toujours

Contents

Preface

There has been an outpouring of books on the Islamic head-scarf lately. The most intellectually impressive is anthropologist Saba Mahmood's *Politics of Piety* (2005), which is an ethnographic study of female mosque goers and activists in Cairo, Egypt. It captures (and buries in academic jargon) the paradox that the headscarf, even if freely chosen, cannot but signify submission, notionally to God, but in reality to men. Most books on Europe are about the mother of all European headscarf controversies, France. Anthropologist John Bowen's *Why the French don't like Headscarves* (2006) confirms what Jürgen Habermas once said, in an informal setting, about American academics at large: 'And then comes an American to clarify everything.' Of all European headscarf books, Bowen's is my favorite. You find in it a crisp synthesis of French republicanism and of the French ('laic') way of dealing with religion which obliterates most of the wordy treatises that have piled up on the topic, especially by French authors. *The Politics of the Veil* (2007), by the noted feminist scholar Joan Wallach Scott, is not trailing far behind. It includes a brilliant (if far-fetched) interpretation of the French headscarf obsession as a 'clash of gender systems', because, not just for Islam but for difference-blind French republicanism too, the female body is prickly disturbing. However, calling the Islamic repression of female flesh 'recognition' and the French exteriorizing of flesh 'denial' is a touch too slick, and one wonders whether the world outside Princeton works that way. The one notable French production on France is *Secularism Meets Islam* (2007), by leading Islam specialist Olivier Roy. It is the best (and deceptively misleading) exculpation of Islam that you can find, written from a sane perspective of 'political liberalism' which is stunningly exotic for a French pen.

So why another headscarf book? With the exception of legal scholar Dominic McGoldrick's *Human Rights and Religion – The Islamic Headscarf Debate in Europe* (2006), few have noticed that other European countries also had headscarf controversies. In Germany, for instance, there has been anti-headscarf legislation almost simultaneously with that of France. This is an obvious invitation to compare – which in fact first raised my interest in the topic. But most of the headscarf books cited above are not just geographically but conceptually limited. Especially the French headscarf books, even when written by American academics, are too parochially French – they fail to see, and at best to take more seriously, that French republicanism is a variant of liberalism. So, in addition to broadening the horizon beyond France, the ambition of this book is to investigate the work that liberalism does in the reception of the headscarf. Liberalism, as John Gray (2000) brilliantly observed, has two faces: that of a modus vivendi for reconciling many ways of life; and that of a way of life in itself – one that is conducted autonomously and rationally. At the risk of simplification, one could say that French republicanism is liberalism as a way of life. Prohibiting the headscarf in the name of republicanism is thus within the ambit of liberalism. This is what all French headscarf books overlook.

Accordingly, the distinct angle of this book is to see the Islamic headscarf as a challenge to liberalism. As liberalism has two faces, two opposite responses to the headscarf are equally possible within its ambit: toleration of the headscarf, as in Britain; or its prohibition, as in France. Comparing France and Britain, this book throws into sharp relief the two liberalisms' difficulties with the headscarf: in its ethical variant (France), liberalism risks to turn into its repressive opposite, whereas in the procedural variant (Britain) liberalism encourages illiberal extremism.

But there is a third possible way to respond to the headscarf, which falls outside the confines of liberalism. I take this to be (in part) the German response, which completes the canvas of cases considered in this book: the Islamic headscarf is selectively rejected in this case because it is Islamic; conversely, the Christian headscarf is accepted because it is part of 'our' culture. There is a difference in kind between the German and the French and British responses: if you are Muslim – the Germans seem to say – you cannot expect to be included on equal terms, because our society is 'Christian–occidental'. The French and British responses to the headscarf are, in different ways, liberal responses: they offer equal terms of inclusion (or of exclusion). The German response is, not in name but in substance, nationalist, in that it draws a particularistic distinction between 'us' and 'them' as differently situated groups that cannot mix. The reader will now guess where the author stands on the headscarf debates: he finds the British and French responses equally legitimate (though one may quarrel about which one has less desirable consequences), yet he finds the German response deeply wanting in a Europe which fifteen million Muslims call home and which may fashion itself as a Christian Club only at its own peril.

This book continues my long-standing interest in the role of liberalism in western states' immigration, citizenship, and ethnic minority (as a shorthand: membership) policies. In *Selecting by Origin: Ethnic Migration in the Liberal State* (2005), I have explicated how liberalism has made western states' immigration policies less ethnically and racially discriminatory and thus more universalistic in the past half-century. In the present book I turn to liberalism's home ground, which is the containment of religious conflict. The book builds and expands on a recent article of mine, 'State neutrality and Islamic headscarf laws in France and Germany' (2007a). The article contrasts neutrality and multicultural recognition as opposite ways of dealing with cultural difference. The present book is more about variants of liberalism and their impact on the reception of Islam in Europe.

Moreover, as is flagged by the title, I take the headscarf as a 'mirror of identity' which forces the French, the British, and the Germans to see who they are and to rethink the kinds of societies and public institutions they want to have. The liberal and the national themes are closely intertwined: as the headscarf is an affront to liberal values, the identities reflected in it are liberal identities. Even the German self-definition as 'Christian–occidental' is a liberal identity, albeit one that unduly particularizes liberalism by confounding genesis and validity, so that Muslims qua Muslims (that is, qua people with different origins) cannot be part of it.

It is time to stop denying that Islam constitutes a fundamental challenge to liberalism. No matter how liberal states and societies respond to this challenge, they cannot but violate some of their own liberal precepts – repress religious liberties, as in the French and German banning of the headscarf, or encourage illiberal views and practices, which seems to be the result of British toleration.

I would like to thank the Swiss Foundation for Population, Migration, and Environment (PME) for funding this research from April 2007 on. In this period, Leyla Arslan provided helpful research assistance. This is the first part of a larger PME-funded project with John Torpey (CUNY, Graduate Center) which compares the institutional accommodation of Islam in North America and western Europe.

Paris, February 2008

1 The Islamic Headscarf in Western Europe

Islamic headscarf controversy is no longer a peculiarity of France, whose classic Foulard Affair dates back to 1989. In fact, there is no country in western Europe today which does not have its own headscarf controversy.[1] And, one must add, each country has the headscarf controversy it deserves. In France, the innocuous bandanna has stirred debate for two decades now, a debate culminating in the 2004 law against 'ostensible' religious symbols in public schools. In Britain, which had long considered itself immune to the religious cloth struggles of the continent, it is the more extreme wear of the *jilbab* and *niqab*[2] that has recently tested the limits of its multicultural leanings. The Netherlands, site of Europe's most draconian retreat from multiculturalism, has predictably attempted the most draconian anti-veiling measure of all, proposing a law in 2006 that would prohibit the wearing of the face-covering veil in all public places (though it never went beyond the conceptual stage). More moderately, Germany, in a series of sub-federal *Länder* laws passed in 2004 and 2005, prohibited public school teachers from dressing up religiously, but made a curious exemption for the adherents of the Christian faith.

The European proliferation of headscarf controversies raises at least two questions. First, why is there controversy at all? Secondly, why has it gone to different lengths in different countries? Both questions require different frames of reference. On the side of commonalities, there are certain liberal norms, most notably gender equality, which seem to be violated by the 'submissive' headscarf. On the side of variation,

1

national legacies of relating religion to the state fare centrally, among other factors.

However, at a deeper level still, the Islamic headscarf functions as mirror of identity which forces the Europeans to see who they are and to rethink the kinds of public institutions and societies they wish to have. Not by accident, the recent headscarf controversies coincide with a busy reassessment of the meaning of 'French', 'German', 'British' or 'Dutch' and with mobilizing law and public policy to make immigrants and ethnic minorities fit these definitions (see Joppke 2007b, 2008). As the challenge is to central precepts of liberal states and societies – the neutrality of the state, individual autonomy, and equality between men and women – it is no wonder that the responses tend to be identical as well: 'we', the French, German, British and Dutch, are first and foremost 'liberal', cherishing the equality of women and the autonomy of the self, and this may require excluding and banishing from the public realm the affront to liberal self-definition for which the Islamic headscarf stands today above all. Liberalism now does the 'exclusionary' work which, at an earlier time, had been done by racism or nationalism (on exclusionary nationalism, see Marx 2003). This does not mean that assertive liberalism does not come in distinct national colors – 'republican' in France, 'Christian–occidental' in Germany, 'multicultural' in Britain – up to a point where liberalism may submerge under resurgent nationalism. The submersion of liberalism by nationalism seems to have happened, in different ways, in France and Germany, reflected in their respective anti-headscarf laws. But notably it has not happened in Britain, where what has come under attack is not the Islamic headscarf as such, but only a particularly extreme version of it.

But why is it only European countries, not the United States or Canada or Australia, that have headscarf controversies? Obviously a facile equation of headscarf opposition with assertive liberalism will not do, because then one would expect similar (if not more) conflict in these other liberal places. With respect to the United States, in the American headscarf controversy that never was, an Oklahoma school district which had excluded a Muslim headscarf girl in March 2004 was immediately opposed by the Federal Department of Justice, which would 'not tolerate discrimination against Muslims or any other religious group' because 'such intolerance is un-American, and [. . .] morally despicable'.[3] This is part of the larger paradox that the country which, together with Israel, is the most reviled one in the Muslim world has no domestic problem with integrating Muslim minorities. Instead, as Aristide Zolberg and Long Litt Woon (1999) memorably pointed out, 'Spanish' is to the US what 'Islam' is to Europe on the immigrant and ethnic minority integration front. The reasons for this are manifold and can only be touched on briefly here (for a good overview, see Foner and Alba 2007).

First, state and religion are more strictly separated in the US than in Europe – even than in France, where Christianity and Judaism enjoyed certain privileges and corporate status which have only recently – and haltingly – expanded to Islam. Secondly, in a curious counterpoint to this, European societies have become thoroughly secularized in the past half-century or so, now constituting the main exception to religious revivalisms around the world. By contrast, American society has become even more religious over time, up to a point of becoming the most religious society of the western world. In such a pious setting, Muslims' religious claims raise fewer eyebrows than in Europe. Finally and perhaps most importantly, there is less potential in the United States than in Europe for the Islamic headscarf to become a 'stigma symbol' (Göle 2003) through which a sign of oppression is re-fashioned into one of resistance. This is because Muslims in the US are not as socio-economically deprived as in Europe. Their smaller numbers, dispersed settlement, and elevated socio-economic status and education make American immigrant Muslims less attuned to the globally politicized Islam which is, ultimately, the driving force behind the proliferation of the headscarf (see Skerry 2006).

The Meanings of the Headscarf

If some western societies like the United States have no problem with the headscarf, on the part of organized Islam and many a Muslim the headscarf seems to carry a broadly anti-western meaning. Hans Küng, in his monumental study of Islam (2004: 739), even flatly holds that the headscarf is a 'symbol of religious–political conviction [. . .] for Islam and against the secular state'. This has not always been so. Originally the Islamic headscarf bore neither political nor religious meaning. It was instead a symbol of status which stood for the 'protection of the private sphere of the wives of Mohammad' (Küng 2004: 738). Accordingly, the Koranic prescriptions for the female wardrobe are in terms of 'societal conventions', not of 'religious obligations' (ibid.). This situation has changed with the headscarf revival in Iran and in the Middle East a quarter-century ago, which in the meantime has caught up with the young second and third-generation Muslims across Europe. Here is how a noted anthropologist reflected on more than twenty years of field-work in Egypt: 'I cannot think of a single woman I know, from the poorest rural to the most educated cosmopolitan, who has ever expressed envy of US women, women they tend to perceive as bereft of community, vulnerable to sexual violence and social anomie, driven by individual success rather than morality, or strangely disrespectful of God' (Abu-Lughod 2002: 788).

In one of the first studies of the headscarf revival, observing a 'new Egyptian woman', college educated or in the process of becoming so but 'completely "veiled"' – face and body', Fadwa El Guindi (1981) noted that the 'immodesty' which the veil repudiates is 'associated with westernism' (quotes from p. 465 and 476). Is it then far-fetched if, some twenty years later, a French president perceived the Islamic headscarf as a 'kind of aggression'?[4] Grosso modo, today's Islamic headscarf stands for the rejection of 'western materialism, commercialism, and values' (El Guindi 2001: 110) whether this is intended by its wearer or not, and this is why there has been controversy surrounding it.

However, the Islamic headscarf is a provocation which cannot be suppressed unless the West denies its own values, such as tolerance and religious freedoms. This is the central paradox of all headscarf controversies: the headscarf is an affront to liberal values, but its suppression is illiberal also and as such a denial of these same values.

It has become commonplace to stress the modernity of the headscarf, conceiving of it not as something imposed by traditionalist milieux but as a self-chosen sign of female emancipation (the paradigmatic statement of this view is Göle 1996). But it is a highly truncated kind of modernity, which has been well captured in Saba Mahmood's ethnography of the women's mosque movement in Egypt (Mahmood 2005). This study gives profound insight into the 'Islamic revival', which is at the same time modern, anti-western, and in search of a pure, de-ethnicized essence of Islam. The women's mosque movement, which began in the 1980s, has grown out of opposition to an increasing 'secularization' and 'westernization' of Egyptian society as a result of which Islam had been reduced to 'custom and folklore' (Mahmood 2005: 44). As a female Mosque activist put it, the point was to 'make our daily lives congruent with our religion' instead (ibid., p. 45). And the true essence of this religion was to be retrieved from its original revelation, the Koran. As archaic as it sounds, the prerequisite for this was a modicum of modernity – public education and urbanization that made 'modern Muslim citizens [. . .] well versed in doctrinal arguments [. . .] hitherto confined to [. . .] religious specialists' (p. 79). But particularly the fact that *women* made these claims attests to the modernity of the Islamic revival: reference to a pure Islam was these women's way of claiming a place in public, outside their home.

However, the rub is that pure Islam, at least in the form it has been retrieved by the revival, underwrites patriarchy. As Mahmood concedes, 'piety' (which is the ethos of the female mosque movement) 'and male superiority are ineluctably intertwined' (p. 175). And the most pertinent sign of male superiority is the headscarf itself. The famous headscarf verse of the Koran prescribes: 'Enjoin believing women to turn their eyes away from temptation and to preserve their chastity; not to display their adornments [. . .] to draw their veils over their bosoms and not to display their finery except to their husbands (and other male kin).'[5] This entails the reduction of women to their sexuality, which represents a 'danger [. . .] to the sanctity

of the Muslim community' (Mahmood 2005: 111). The function of the headscarf is to limit and confine this sexuality to
its rightful owner, the husband (although all male relatives are
allowed to see the unveiled woman too). This ownership is
established through the overall assumption that men are the
natural guardians of women. Surah 4(34) of the Koran states:
'Men have authority over women because God has made the
one superior to the other, and because they spend their wealth
to maintain them. Good women are obedient [. . .] As for those
from whom you fear disobedience, admonish them, forsake
them in beds apart, and beat them' (The Koran 2003: 64). To
the degree that women 'choose' a pious life, which is one
obedient to the Koranic God, they enter a condition which even
a sympathetic observer like Saba Mahmood finds structurally
akin to that of a 'voluntary slave' (2005: 149): they choose
subordination.

Having established that Islam, as understood within the
'politics of piety', entails the subordination of women,
Mahmood helps herself out of the dilemma thus created by
arguing, in learned but arcane prose, that heteronomy is part
of the human condition. Quoting Aristotle and Foucault, she
holds that there cannot be a 'self' before 'socially prescribed
forms of behavior', so that the autonomous self so dear to the
West is a mirage, an Enlightenment fiction. This yields an
interesting perspective on the 'politics of piety': the latter is *not*
a politics of identity, as one might think, because ritual practice, in the view of the practitioner, is a tool for the *creation* of
the self, and hence cannot be its *expression*. But this does not
change the fact that female subordination and affirmation of
patriarchy is still the outcome. As Mahmood (2001) concedes,
'the very idioms that women use to assert their presence in
previously male-defined spheres are *also* those that secure
their subordination' (p. 205). Nilüfer Göle's celebrated study
of the 1980s Islamic veiling movement of female university
students in Turkey comes to the same conclusion: 'With the
act of veiling women perform a political statement against
Western modernism, yet at the same time they seem to accept
the male domination that rests their own invisibility and their
confinement to the private sphere' (Göle 1996: 136).

The modern veiling movement's claim to return to a 'golden age' of Islam, in which there was 'equality between women and men' (ibid., pp. 104–8), is futile: this age never existed. As Leila Ahmed showed in her authoritative study on women and gender in Islam, the moment at which classic Islamic law was formulated 'was a singularly unpropitious one for women' (Ahmed 1992: 100). The early Muslim conquests led to a 'continuity and accentuation of the life-styles already in place' in the conquered lands of Mesopotamia, among which a 'fierce misogyny' stood out (p. 35). If one adds that Islam is originally, as Max Weber put it memorably, a religion of 'world-conquering warrior(s)' (Weber 1976: 311), it is no surprise that 'the feminine dimension of experience is excluded' from it, to quote the sociologist of religion Robert Bellah (1970: 155). This picture of Islam contrasts to that of Christianity (more precisely, of Catholicism), where the masculinity of the Old Testament God is loosened up by 'the person of Mary' (ibid.). E. Çelebi, a Turkish writer famous in his own time, who was visiting Vienna in 1665 as part of an Ottoman diplomatic mission, observed: 'In this country and in general in the lands of the unbelievers, women have the main say. They are honored and respected out of love for Mother Mary' (quoted in Lewis 2002: 65). By contrast, Robert Bellah finds that a certain machismo is inherent in Islam, in that '(t)he second-class position of women has been reflected in an inability by men to accept the feminine aspects of their own personalities' (Bellah 1970: 164).

Comparing Christianity and Islam, Bernard Lewis similarly finds that the 'status of women' is 'probably the most profound single difference between the two civilizations' (Lewis 2002: 67). Although conceding that Islam is inherently 'an egalitarian religion' in which 'the actions and utterances of the Prophet [. . .] are overwhelmingly against privilege by descent, by birth, by status, or even by race' (p. 82), Lewis identifies three groups who are excluded from Islam's penchant for equality: unbelievers, slaves, and women. And women are the 'worst-placed of the three' (p. 67), because neither conversion nor abolition is on offer for them.

It is therefore no wonder that the subordination of women has been at the center of the western critique of Islam ever since colonial times, the veil being the most obvious symbol of this subordination. Of course, this critique was strikingly hypocritical. Leila Ahmed cites the case of Lord Cromer, who indicted veiling and segregation in colonized Egypt, but back home in England was the president (and a founding member) of the Men's League for Opposing Women's Suffrage (Ahmed 1992: 153). As Ahmed bitingly states, 'the Victorian colonial paternalistic establishment appropriated the language of feminism in the service of its assault on the religions and cultures of Other men' (p. 152). In turn, to the degree that 'the occupier was bent on unveiling' Muslim society, as Frantz Fanon put it with respect to the French in Algeria, the veil took on the new meaning of resistance, which it would recover in the 1980s Islamic revival, with the ironic implication that 'it is Western discourse that in the first place determined the new meanings of the veil' (quoted ibid., p.164). The Islamic headscarf has evidently been a central stake of conflict ever since the West has encountered Islam. Accordingly, a contemporary critic of 'colonial feminism' refers to Lord Cromer to denounce the western attacks on the Islamic headscarf, in the Taliban's Afghanistan and elsewhere, as 'white men saving brown women from brown men' (Abu-Lughod 2002). As the Columbia University anthropologist put it rather slickly: 'We need to have as little dogmatic faith in secular humanism as in Islamism, and as open a mind to the complex possibilities of human projects undertaken in one tradition as the other' (p. 789).

There is no doubt that 'secular humanism' has its own dark history with respect to women. The Greco-Roman and Jewish-Christian traditions are not devoid of hierarchical thinking in gender relations, to say the least – equating maleness with reason and womanhood with nature, as they did, and subordinating the latter to the former. Leila Ahmed quotes Aristotle claiming, in the *Politics*, that the rule of man over woman is like the rule of 'soul over the body, and of the mind and the rational element over the passionate' (Ahmed 1992: 29). And she observes that Augustine failed 'to see what use woman can be to men [. . .] if one excludes the function of bearing children' (ibid., 36).

However, the difference seems to be that 'secular human-ism' could gradually rid itself of such views, whereas 'Islamism' (to use Abu-Lughod's terms) did not. Ernest Gellner (1992: 6) located this difference in Islam's penchant for being 'secularization-resistant'. To explain this resistance, one has to consider two elements of Islam: extreme scripturalism and monism. With respect to scripturalism, more than the preced-ing two monotheisms, Judaism and Christianity, 'Islam is a founded religion, claiming to complete and round off the Abrahamic tradition and its Prophets, and to do so with final-ity' (ibid). Mohammad is the *last* prophet, through whom God has spoken to humankind *for the last time* (Schluchter 1991: 299). There is to be no addition, divine or human, to the revela-tion of God's word in the Koran. Being 'revealed not enacted' (Lewis 1993: 43), Islamic law cannot be changed in any way, and least of all by human beings. Of course, a sacred script is a feature of all western monotheisms, which are religions of the book, Islam only being the most completely developed variant. The difference is that Koran is 'God's word turned into a book' (Küng 2004: 93), whereas the Bible has been 'written on earth' (p. 620) and its human authorship has never been put in question by Jewish or Christian virtuosi. The claim that the Koran was written by humans, as raised by the contempo-rary Iranian Islamic thinker Abdolkarim Soroush, is heresy within Islam (see Nirumand 2008). The return to the original script is one of the elements of 'fundamentalism' (see Marty 2001) – which was invented, of course, by Protestants in early twentieth-century America. Islam is inherently geared to such a stance still more than its Abrahamite sister religions because of the 'inimitable, inviolate, inerrant, and incontro-vertible' nature of the Koran as 'Divine Discourse' (Barlas 2002: 33).

A second reason for Islam's resistance to secularization is monism. 'Islam is the blueprint of a social order', as Ernest Gellner opened his famous study on *Muslim Society* (1981: 1). There is no separation in Islam between state and religion, and 'theocracy' is built in its structure (Küng 2004: 207). By contrast, a key feature of Christianity is dualism, the separa-tion of worldly and heavenly spheres, expressed in Jesus' famous admonition in the Book of Matthew (22, 15–34) to 'render to Cesar what is due to Cesar and to God what is due to God', and reiterated in Augustine's (however polemic) distinction between the 'city of God' and the 'city of man'. This dualism made Christianity, as the French historian of religion Marcel Gauchet put it, the 'religion for departing from all religion' (Gauchet 1997: 4), that is, of embarking on the road to secularization. By contrast, Islam, while being the most universalistic and egalitarian of monotheisms – and in this sense, paradoxically, the 'closest to modernity' (Gellner 1981: 7) – does not allow for a separation of spheres within society, one of it closer to God than the others. '[S]uch a segregation', writes Gellner (p. 1), 'would contradict both the symmetry or equality of access, and the requirement of pervasive implementation of the rules.' Accordingly, Islam has no clergy or church, but also no separate sphere of mundane society from which there could arise an impulse for change. The 'greater social pervasiveness of Islam' (p. 2) is due to the conceptual completeness and finality of the divine message. But it is also due to the empirical fact that the political success of Islam in the time of the Prophet was rapid and successful, so that a division between worldly and divine powers did not arise in the first place.

Being resistant to secularization in these two ways, through extreme scripturalism and monism, Islam forces its believers to bow to the mores of the eighth-century society which is perpetually frozen in it and one of whose features happens to be the subordinate status of women. Certainly, according to the Koran men and women are equal before God because both are created by God; but it does not follow from this that men and women are equal among themselves. Hans Küng summarizes the conventional wisdom (2004: 204): 'It is unwarranted to speak about equality between man and woman in the Koran. The privileges of the man in a patriarchic, extended family that consists of the father, his sons, and their families, remain untouched.'

Against the mainstream view that Islam endorses patriarchy, Asma Barlas (2002) has eloquently argued that 'the teachings of the Qur'ān are radically egalitarian and even antipatriarchal' (p. 93). But, she submits, this is a 'theological defense', premised on the notion that 'how we think about and read God's Speech cannot be divorced from what we believe about God' (p. 204). Accordingly, if one believes that the Koran is 'God's Self-Disclosure', the attribution of injustice or patriarchy to Him would undercut His 'Divine Unity, Justness, and Incomparability' (p. 13). This theological defense is akin to Christian Morgenstern's sarcastic poetry line 'that which must not, can not be' (*nicht sein kann, was nicht sein darf*). It is safe to say that it does not have many followers in Islam. And it raises the thorny question, known to the students of Marx and Marxism, of how the Koran's 'inherently antipatriarchal' stance (p. 2) could have been so completely misunderstood, even turned into the exact opposite, by most interpreters and believers over the centuries (a question discussed with admirable integrity on pp. 205–10).

More importantly for our purposes, Asma Barlas' 'unreading' of patriarchy in the Koran does not include an egalitarian reading of the headscarf. In her view, there are two concepts of the veil in the Koran: one specific and one general. The *specific*, sociologically contingent concept, said to be expressed, for instance, in the famous headscarf verse quoted above, is not formulated in terms of a religious proscription and of a principled concealment of dangerous female flesh, into which it has been turned by the Islamic mainstream. Instead, its original purpose is merely instrumental, to protect free Muslim women from non-Muslim men in a slave-owning *Jāhilī* (non-Muslim) society, where unveiled women in public were taken to be slave prostitutes and thus fair game (pp. 53–8). The *general*, more genuinely religious concept either refers to a virtual veil which is a matter of how to direct one's eyes and gaze more than of not being seen; or – if indeed it involves body and dress – it refers to a generic modesty of dress which is addressed to women *and* men alike and which may be realized in many ways (pp. 158–60). From the latter concept, an *asymmetric* obligation (not applying to men) for *this* solution to modesty (the veil) could never be derived. Accordingly, if contemporary Muslim women insist on the veil as a matter of religious obligation, it is an obligation which cannot be found as such in Islam's central script and is entirely construed by the conservative mainstream in terms of a 'proof of female immorality and inferiority' (p. 57). From Barlas' analysis there follows that, however freely chosen, the veil is ultimately a captive to patriarchy.

Next to stressing its modernity, it has also become commonplace to stress the multiplicity of meanings and motivations attached to the Islamic headscarf. Again, this obscures the religious baggage that necessarily goes with it, which seems to enshrine the subordinate status of women. Certainly, it is a liberal precept that the meaning of religion cannot be objectively decreed but is in the eye of the beholder. However, not anything goes, as not even a feminist reading of Islam (as in Barlas 2002) could absolve the headscarf of its patriarchal underpinnings.

The different meanings of the veil are perhaps best studied in the European country which had the biggest problem with it: France. The pioneering work by Françoise Gaspard and Farhad Khosrokhavar (1995: 34–69) distinguishes between three meanings of the headscarf. The least controversial is the 'veil of the immigrant', which signifies the 'permanence of the identity of origin' (p. 34). The traditionalist veil of the mature or elderly Muslim woman (call it *le voile des mamans*)[6] appears wherever there is immigration from Muslim countries. It 'marks the permanence of the immemorial principles of the country of origin in the face of the traumatisms of change and of transplantation into a different society' (p. 35). Controversy arose only around a second veil, the 'veil of the adolescent', which is imposed by parents as a sign of modesty and for the purpose of controlling their daughters' sexuality. Interestingly, though, this is also the first veil to bear emancipating possibilities, as it allows the Muslim girl to 'go out' (p. 37) and be protected from harassment by her male environment, be it that of her peers in the *banlieues* or that of her family. It is the veil that allows a Muslim girl to do the things that the anomic ghetto culture of her male peers or the traditionalist family may despise – to attend school and learn, and thus prepare for a successful life outside home, which is otherwise foreclosed to Muslim women. As Gaspard and Khosrokhavar put it, the 'veil of the adolescent' gives 'to parents the illusion of continuity while in fact it marks discontinuity: it allows the passage to *altérité (la modernité)* under the pretext of *identité (la tradition)*' (p. 44). This veil is not unlike the 'mobile homes' identified by Lila Abu-Lughod in Islamic states, which allow 'women to move out of segregated living spaces while still observing the basic moral requirements of separating and protecting women from unrelated men' (2002: 785).

The third and most interesting, because most paradoxical, type is the 'autonomous veil' (labeled *voile revendiqué*). This veil is freely chosen, and the expression of an 'Islamic identity' on the part of assertive young second-generation Muslims, aged between 16 and 25 (Gaspard and Khosrokhavar 1995: 47). As the authors note, the autonomous veil is often donned by those who are most 'integrated' into French society through their studies or through their lower middle-class standing. In fact, Gaspard and Khosrokhavar attribute to the autonomous veil 'the desire to be French and Muslim, modern and veiled, autonomous and dressed in the Islamic way' (p. 47). The autonomous veil comes with further variations, as a statement of protest 'against racism' (p. 49) or as a religious statement spurred by the Islamic revival discussed above, which has most recently gained strength with the spreading of Salafi fundamentalism.[7] The autonomous veil has by now become the orthodoxy of French sociology. Further studies, especially by students of Khosrokhavar at the Ecole des Hautes Etudes en Sciences Sociales (EHESS), zoomed in on the autonomous veil's dualism of wanting to be French and Islamic at the same time (Venel 1999; Weibel 2000).

As Joan W. Scott argued in a superb account of the French headscarf controversy, the 'polysemy' of the veil entails 'a deliberate obfuscation of meaning'; and she surmises that the whole point of the French government's legislating against it, in 2004, was to contain the veil's 'position as an unstable signifier' (Scott 2005: 117–19). Perhaps – except that such a conclusion is a bit too cavalier about a stubbornly objective dimension of the veil, which is religious. Despite the multiplicity of meanings that may be attached to it, from traditionalism to (pragmatically endured) imposition to autonomous choice, the

Islamic headscarf can never be abstracted from the religious dimension. Otherwise it would be just fashion. And the religious core of the headscarf points to the subordinate status of women. Accordingly, Jytte Klausen (2005), who is otherwise hopeful about the rise of a liberal-minded 'European Islam' (p. 205), concedes: 'The frequently made argument that women must cover up to prove themselves "chaste" and "pure" illustrates that it *is* intended as a restriction on women's sexual freedom. If women's bodies must be hidden because they are distracting to men or offensive, it *does* connote female inferiority' (p. 186). But it is a small step from here to agreeing with Bernard Stasi, whose report laid the grounds for the 2004 French anti-headscarf law, that '[o]bjectively the veil stands for the alienation of women' (quoted in Scott 2005: 116). In the French context, the *banlieue* Muslim women's movement '*Ni putes ni soumises*', led by Fadela Amara, takes an identical stance. While acknowledging that the veil may help to protect young Muslim females from aggression by the *garçons de la cité* (boys of the suburbs), the movement's point is to debunk the veil as a sign of the subordination of women: 'Let us not forget that (the veil) is above all a tool of oppression, of alienation, of discrimination, an instrument of the power of men over women' (Amara 2003: 79).

The Liberal State Meets the Islamic Headscarf

So the burden of proof is on those who deny that the Islamic headscarf implies the subordination of women and thus violates a core liberal value. However, this does not provide a license for the liberal state to legislate against the headscarf. After all, most religions are illiberal, almost by definition, as they dwarf the individual before God. More concretely, to wear a headscarf falls within the ambit of religious freedom, which is *also* protected in the liberal state. Moreover, to determine the meaning of religion and its behavioral implications falls entirely outside the competence of the liberal state (at least as long as no rights of third parties are impaired). In this sense, the state has to be agnostic as to whether Islam *really* prescribes the veil for women. Accordingly, the veil, through the very fact of being considered a religious symbol by the woman donning it, falls within the ambit of religious liberty rights.

It has been a staple of high-court jurisdiction around the western world that what religion is and what it implies can only be determined by those who believe in it. For instance, when having to decide whether 'Jehova's Witnesses' was a legitimate religion, to be recognized by the state on an equal level with the established religions, the German Constitutional Court determined: 'The religiously and ideologically neutral state must not evaluate belief and creed [*Glauben und Lehre*].'[8] Article 4 of the German Basic Law, which stipulates the 'inviolability' of the 'freedom of belief', is generally held to prevent the state from qualifying religious beliefs as 'right' or 'wrong', leaving this to the believer herself (Hillgruber 1999: 541). In the same vein, the European Court of Human Rights held that the right to freedom of religion, protected in Article 9 of the European Convention on Human Rights (ECHR), 'excludes assessment by the State of the legitimacy of religious beliefs or the ways in which those beliefs are expressed' (quoted in McGoldrick 2006: 8). And, outside Europe, when the South African Supreme Court had to decide whether the use of cannabis by a Rastafarian was protected by his constitutional right to freedom of religion, it decreed as follows: '[A]s a general matter, the court should not be concerned with questions whether, as a matter of religious doctrine, a particular practice is central to the religion. Religion is a matter of faith and belief [. . .] [which enjoy] the protection guaranteed by the right to freedom of religion' (ibid., 10). So, when having to decide whether wearing a headscarf is a religious obligation and hence is protected by the right to religious freedom, European courts abstained from any interpretation, not to mention evaluation, of the Koran, because this would violate the liberal state's general policy of neutrality towards religious affairs (ibid., 9).

At the same time, a strict neutral stance is equally self-defeating, because it would open the door for the capricious labeling as 'religious' of actions with other than religious motives, whose sole purpose is seeking cover by the law. Accordingly, there is a concurrent strand of European courts going into substantive discussions of when a religion is and what it prescribes. At the organizational level, a decision has to be made whether, say, Christian Scientology is 'just marketing a science-fiction narrative' or it 'represents a religious creed' (Heinig and Morlok 2003: 778). At the individual level, a threshold definition of an action as 'religious' (and not just sectarian or lunatic) has to be made, so that the action in question may fall within the ambit of constitutional religious liberty clauses. Such a definition must be based on a minimal 'objective' common ground, separate and apart from the 'subjective' definitions of any actors. Courts have helped themselves out of the dilemma of identifying objectively what is inherently subjective by asking religious authorities what a particular religion prescribes in behavioral terms – which in the case of Islam is rarely consensual, so that courts are thrown back to the exit position and forced to define what is not up to them to define.

Nevertheless, as Olivier Roy (2005) pointed out in a lucid discussion of secularism confronting Islam, the liberal state must never intervene in and control religious dogma, and its action toward religion must occur in other terms – for instance of public order, of the interest of third parties, and the like. Reiterating 'political liberalism' à la Rawls (1993), which is astonishing for a French author, Roy stipulates that consent in a liberal state is never substantive, in terms of 'common values', but only procedural, in terms of 'common rules of the game' (Roy 2005: 68). Accordingly, even if Islam may be structurally resistant to secularization, it is still the wrong thing (a 'methodological fault', says Roy, p. 69) to ask it to become secularized. As Roy rightly reminds us, the Catholic Church rejected laicity and the republic in France throughout the nineteenth century, and only twenty years after its passing did the Church accept the 1905 Law on Laicity, which privatizes religion in France. More generally, not before the Second Vatican Council in the 1960s did the Catholic Church make peace with the secularized world. And, still today, the Catholic Church believes in an 'objective and universal truth' (Cardinal

Ratzinger, quoted in Roy, p. 68, n.1) which is above political law – otherwise why would it continue to oppose abortion? Surely it would be hypocritical to deny Islam the autonomy of dogma and the principle of non-interference which have marked the European states' approach to their historically established religions.

As we shall see in the following chapters, courts, especially constitutional courts, have been a major actor in all European headscarf controversies, and in most cases they upheld religious liberty claims against restrictive governments. In fact these controversies are a prime example of constitutional politics in which higher courts have clashed with democratic governments and which has become a hallmark of politics throughout western states, especially where minorities are involved (for Europe, see Stone Sweet 2000).

To understand fully the role of constitutional politics, we need to locate headscarf controversies more precisely within the overall accommodation of Islam in western Europe. This accommodation has occurred along two separate tracks, one organizational and another individual. Each track follows a different logic and allows for a different speed. The organizational track follows the logic of corporatism: the task is to integrate Islam as a corporate actor into already established state-church regimes, which so far included only the religions historically established in society. The individual track follows the logic of individual rights: all modern constitutions include religious liberty clauses, which naturally do not stop short of Muslim believers.

The two tracks allow for different speeds. The individual track immediately applies wherever constitutional religious liberties are violated. Accordingly, the integration of Islam has been, first and foremost – and to a still largely unacknowledged degree – promoted by higher courts, which for several decades now have allowed exemptions from religiously incensed parts of the public school curriculum, have modified laws on the slaughtering of animals to accommodate religious diet, and, yes, have often revoked exclusions from school or from work on account of wearing a headscarf – to list only a few more noted areas of legal intervention.

By contrast, accommodation on the organizational track has generally been much slower, because of the historical inertia of established state-church regimes. But there has been a remarkable trend in recent years, in France, Britain, and Germany among other European countries, for the state to further proactively the incorporation of Islam into a quasi-church – if perhaps more out of public order than justice considerations (see Haddad and Golson 2007). The most dramatic expression of this has been the creation of the Conseil Français du Culte Musulman (CFCM) in France, under the Minister of the Interior, Nicolas Sarkozy, in 2003. The main obstacle to such incorporation is not a bias against Islam, but the non-church character of Islam, which is internally divided into sects and by national origins. At deeper level, of course, the very existence of a church, a 'salvation society' separate from mundane society, is the expression of the 'dualism' which is constitutive of Christianity, but not of Islam (Gauchet 1997: 132–4).

The hurdles that stand in the way of a full equality of Islam as organized religion with Christianity are often subtle. In Germany, the challenge for Islam is to be recognized as a 'corporation of public law' (*Körperschaft des öffentlichen Rechts*), which would, for instance, allow an Islamic 'church' to tax its members with the help of the state and to hold religious instruction in schools at the state's expense – to name only the two most visible and highly coveted privileges. While this status was automatically granted in Article 140 of the Basic Law to those religions which had already been such corporations before the founding of the Federal Republic in 1948, any newcomer has first to establish a 'guarantee of permanence' (*Gewähr der Dauer*), defined by their 'inner constitution' and by 'the number of their members'. At a minimum, this makes for an 'increased procedural and argumentative effort' (Gusy 2006: 183) on the part of new religions, Islam included, which the established religions did not face. Up to the present day, Islam's quest to achieve public corporation status, despite repeated attempts, has not proved successful in Germany. But the federal government has recently gone as far as to support confessional Koran instruction in German public schools, which signals a more benign attitude toward clearing some of the organizational and recognition hurdles which still stand in the way (see Bundesministerium des Innern 2008). With respect to the organizational accommodation of Islam, the minimum to say is: the slate can never be clean. Historical state-church regimes have been the unavoidable exit condition for accommodating Islam. And these regimes come in highly variegated forms: strict separation between state and church in France and the United States, the privileging of an official state church in Britain and Scandinavia, and the mixed regimes of Germany and the Netherlands, where the dominant religions in society are granted public recognition and status (see Ferrari 1995). It is therefore all the more astonishing that these regimes have all made a similar headway in accommodating organized Islam, laic France, which on the face of it is the one most hostile to all religions, no less than the one apparently most Christian, Anglican Britain.

Having said this, the headscarf controversies are located outside the organizational track, namely on the individual track of accommodating Islam. While the two tracks are mutually related in that a recognized status of Islam will certainly help the individual to pursue more effectively her religious claims, the individual track is still to be kept distinct. As it applies irrespective of organizational gains (or lack thereof), the individual track is in principle much faster, stronger, and more reliable, because it is one that the liberal state cannot deny to any of its members. By contrast, the logic of corporatism is asymmetric and non-egalitarian, granting to the major forces and actors of society a privileged role in public life and policy which is denied to smaller groups, who are unable to muster the requisite mass.

However, religious rights along the individual track are not absolute – otherwise there would be no banning of the headscarf. Religious rights find their limits in the rights of other individuals and third parties or in public order considerations of the state. By the same token, in a liberal state the right to wear the headscarf is never an issue in the private sphere. This may be trivial, but it needs to be rendered explicit. The headscarf becomes an issue only in the public sphere, that is, when third parties and their rights and interests are involved. Of course, the dividing line between private and public is drawn differently in different states. In the proposed Dutch 'burka ban', which has been justified by the government as an anti-terrorist measure, 'public' includes physical places where people congregate in large numbers, like cinemas, railway stations, or airports. This is a rather expansive definition of 'public', which tends to annihilate its opposite, 'private'. It has remained the exception and the related measure (for the time being) has not seen the light of day.

The two public settings where the headscarf has typically become an issue are employment and schooling. In the realm of employment, the headscarf brings to a head the employee's right to freedom of religion and the employer's economic interest. Once the courts get involved, such conflicts – even in countries not otherwise known for aggressive multicultural policies, like Germany – have often been resolved in favor of the religious claimant (see Thüsing and Wege 2004; Schiek 2004). For instance the German Federal Labor Court, in a high-profile decision in October 2002, branded as 'unfair dismissal' the firing of a headscarf-wearing female employee of Turkish origin, who had worked in the perfume section of a large department store in a provincial German city. The store manager justified the firing by referring to the headscarf's probable negative impact on sales, particularly in a small town in Hesse, where majority standards in dress did not reflect or include a taste for Muslim headscarves. Interestingly, this was not enough to cross out a fundamental individual right: as the Labor Court decreed, the headscarf-wearing employee could have been moved to a less visible area of the shop, away from the glittery perfume counter. The mere *expectation* of sales losses was not sufficient grounds for dismissal; had the employer been able to *prove* such losses (as he was not), the 'balancing of interests' performed by the court might have led to a different conclusion. These are the (mostly) silent and highly legalistic ways in which the Islamic headscarf has made mighty inroads into western societies.

However, the typical site of headscarf controversies is the public school. This type of conflict may overlap with the employment one in cases where the right of teachers to wear headscarves is involved. This has been the case in Germany, whose headscarf debate has been ignited by an aspiring public school teacher's insistence on wearing the headscarf in the classroom. But the constellation of clashing rights and interests is typically more complex in the public school setting than in the case of mere conflicts at the workplace. This is because more parties are involved and the setting itself has a societal, public-order dimension which is absent in private employment disputes (these are 'public' only in the thin sense of happening outside the home and involving a third party). Here are the rights and interests which have to be considered and reconciled in the case of headscarf conflicts in the public school: the religious rights of headscarf-wearing teachers or students; the negative religious liberties of other students (that is, their right not to be confronted with headscarf-wearing teachers or fellow-students); parental rights (these may also cut both ways – for and against the headscarf); and the mandate of the state to provide an environment which is conducive to learning, the development of the child, and the inculcation of citizenship.

In all the cases considered in this book, headscarf controversies have been located in the world of public schooling, though with significant differences. In Germany, the rights of teachers were at stake: were they allowed full religious freedom, like all other individuals, or was this right constrained for the sake of office-holding – given that public school teachers in Germany are civil servants (*Beamte* and *Beamtinnen*) and thus agents of the state who owe it a special obligation of loyalty in return for significant privileges? By contrast, in France, it was never questioned that teachers were not allowed to wear a headscarf: a headscarf claim on the part of a teacher would appear lunatic and incomprehensible there. Instead, the issue in France was the right of pupils to wear a headscarf. This reflects an ambitious nation-building function of the public school, which is to be a 'republican sanctuary' staying clear of religion and ethnicity. Conversely, in Germany, where the nation-building mandate of schools is much less developed, the right of students to wear headscarves was never in question:

this was considered a matter of private choice, without a public dimension. In England, finally, the issue has revolved around the religious rights of teachers and students alike – however, not with respect to wearing an Islamic headscarf per se but only an extreme version of it, which hides the entire body and face (except the eyes). This kind of cover has raised the sociolinguistic question of the prerequisites for an effective 'face-to-face' communication, as well as the political question of how far a toleration of visible markers of separation should go.

Irrespective of these differences of functional sector and social category at stake, the liberal state never meets the Islamic headscarf as a unitary actor. There is at least a division between courts, which tend to take rights-protecting stances, and the political branches of the state (parliament and executive), where other values and considerations, more oriented towards the collectivity, predominate. One such value is security and public order. It corresponds to an elementary, Hobbesian state function which is having a new lease of life in the age of global terrorism. 'Public order' has been the justification for the proposed '*burka* ban' in the Netherlands.

'Neutrality' is a second value, and a rather more interesting one because more complex and genuinely liberal, which has guided the political (but also legal) response of the state to the Islamic headscarf. It is grounded in a Lockean conception of the state. According to it, the liberal state is to stay out of the 'care of souls' and limit itself to the external protection of private property, broadly understood as endowing the members of society with equal liberty rights. State neutrality has been the solution to the religious wars of sixteenth and seventeenth-century Europe, and its rise is thus identical with the birth of liberalism itself. No wonder that neutrality would resurface in the Islamic headscarf debates, as the main justification of the French and the German state for legislating against the headscarf in the early millennium.

However, justifying headscarf bans on grounds of neutrality is paradoxical: how can the restriction of a liberty be done in the name of liberty? In Germany, the neutrality of the state was seen as being impaired if an agent of the state – a teacher

– were to dress religiously, thus taking a stance which upset the required non-partisanship of the state in religious and ideological (*weltanschaulich*) matters, as well as harming the negative religious right of pupils *not* to be confronted with religion. Although this scratches only the surface of a more complex, even contorted justification for banning the headscarf in Germany, one at least senses how liberty may be restricted for the sake of liberty. In France, where not teachers but students were the target of restriction, it is even less obvious how a headscarf ban could ever be justified through appeal to neutrality: can the neutrality of the state be at risk if students, entirely unrelated to the state but subjected to its rule, dress religiously? Yes, but only if one defines the public school (next to the military, the French state's classic nation-building instrument) as a space to be cleansed from all particularistic (ethnic, racial, religious) origin markers, so that the equal, emancipated citizen can emerge.

'Neutrality' has featured in Islamic headscarf controversies as a polyvalent principle (see Joppke 2007a). On the part of (or on behalf of) individuals, usually aligned with the courts, it *may* be a rights-protecting stance, and as such it was brought forward in defense of the headscarf. According to this stance, French *laïcité* is in the first place a principle which guarantees the religious freedom of the individual, as (implicitly) laid out in Article 1 of the 1905 Law on the Separation of Church and State; and *Neutralität*, German-style, is a mandate for the state to be even-handed when it deals with religion – so that, after having welcomed Christianity and Judaism into the public space, the state could not deny Islam the same privilege. On the other hand, on the part of the political state, neutrality has appeared as a collectivity-oriented stance, securing basic state integrity, perhaps even national unity, in the context of societal pluralism. This may justify keeping Islam (like all other religions) out of the public space, along the lines suggested above.

Interestingly, out of our three cases considered in this book, Britain is the one where 'neutrality' has *not* been a central stake in the headscarf controversy. This is simply because the British state has only peripherally been involved in this dispute. In their provocative political sociology of the state – according to which a 'true' state is one which is autonomous and differentiated from civil society – Bertrand Badie and Pierre Birnbaum noted that one cannot find a state in this sense in Britain: '[I]n Britain [. . .] the political center did not develop into a true state because civil society proved capable of governing itself' (Badie and Birnbaum 1983: 125).[9] Accordingly, the main actors in the British headscarf controversy have been Muslims, the schools being charged with accommodating ever more extreme versions of Islamic dress, and the courts having to adjudicate the conflict – but never 'the state'. Epitomizing the British state's hands-off posture, Prime Minister Tony Blair, when asked to comment on the emergent headscarf controversy in 2006, simply responded that he was not the right person to address: 'Issues such as these are matters of personal views, not government policies', to be 'resolved locally'.[10] That was a stance which had to be reluctantly abandoned once the extreme headscarf became a symbol of the refusal to integrate. But all that 'the state' in Britain ever pronounced on the matter was a 'consultation document' issued by the ministry of education which allows schools to restrict extreme Islamic dress for the sake of 'health, safety and the protection of the rights and freedoms of others'.[11] In essence, the British state declared the headscarf no matter of the state, relegating the issue back to the local school – and perhaps wisely so.

However, even in Britain the Islamic headscarf eventually brought up 'the question of the very unity of our nation', as Shadow Home Minister David Davis put it.[12] This statement points to a third justification for the state to reject the headscarf, next to public order and neutrality: according to it, the headscarf is an affront to national self-definition. As a well-known Muslim intellectual articulated this theme, 'there is such a thing as British society', which sets limits to 'privacy and individual choice'.[13] By making a 'visible statement of separation and of difference' (to quote Jack Straw's indictment of the niqab)[14], the headscarf inevitably raised the question of what it is that unites and integrates a national society. In other words the headscarf, in whatever variant, functioned as a mirror of identity. At an individual level, the logic of this was neatly experienced by a 'fortysomething mother' encountering a fully veiled woman, in a carpeted English train compartment, who suddenly made her 'feel as tarty and sexually provocative as a p3 girl': 'It's not a nice sensation – to feel judged for wearing your own clothing in your own country.'[15]

If the veil brings awareness of 'your own clothing in your own country', one might be tempted to conclude that mere nationalism, a factual insistence on 'this is how we do things here', has ultimately stirred the rejection of the Islamic headscarf. Perhaps it has, in some quarters; but as a blanket statement this is wrong. It misses the crucial element of liberalism, which is everywhere (however hypocritically) constitutive of the opposition to the headscarf, and which is also constitutive of all the attempts at national self-definition that have been made in Europe's great debate surrounding Muslim integration (see Joppke 2008). Note, again, that it is not baggy trousers, piercing, or tattoos, but a cloth that stands for the restriction of freedom that is singled out for regulation. In the words of 'enlightenment fundamentalist'[16] Hirsi Ali, the veil is '[a] constant reminder to the outside world of a stifling morality that makes Muslim men the owners of women and obliges them to prevent their mothers, sisters, aunts, sisters-in-law, cousins, nieces, and wives from having sexual contact'.[17]

Outlook

The forthcoming comparison between headscarf controversies in France, Germany, and Britain seeks to do justice to the common liberal themes articulated in them as well as to the distinct national inflections or idioms in which these controversies have been conducted. In France, the national idiom has been that of *laïcité* and republicanism; in Germany, that of 'open neutrality' and Christian–occidental self-definition; in Britain, that of liberal multiculturalism. However, for all these differences, headscarf restrictions were eventually imposed everywhere – by means of parliamentary laws in France and Germany, and by means of High Court rules affirming the right of schools to exclude extreme Islamic dress in Britain.

To calibrate these restrictions, a third consideration must step in: 'whose' or 'which' headscarf is at issue? In France, it is the headscarf of the pupil, which makes for the most far-reaching and momentous of all headscarf restrictions in Europe. In Germany, at issue is only the headscarf of public school teachers, who, as civil servants, are agents of the same state that issues the restriction. In Britain, the Islamic headscarf as such continues to be tolerated for students and teachers alike, but not the extreme version of it, which has been found to obstruct the school's educational mandate.

A fourth consideration rounds up the comparison. Which public institution is processing headscarf claims? The German and French cases will confirm a logic of constitutional politics: headscarf laws are a political backlash against the liberal toleration of headscarves, which had previously taken hold in the legal systems of both countries. Only in Britain, where the state has largely kept out of the headscarf conflict, this logic does not apply: both toleration *and* restriction have emerged from the courts.

2 The Pupil's Headscarf in Republican France

To call the Islamic headscarf a 'mirror of identity' is nowhere more appropriate than in the case of France, the mother of all headscarf controversies. Rather innocuous bandannas worn by a tiny number of pupils in a few *banlieue* schools,[1] objects which in other parts of Europe would have been either overlooked or considered protected by religious liberty rights, stirred a debate over the fundamentals of 'republican' identity and integration, and the dangerous cloth was eventually prevailed upon with the heaviest of guns at the state's disposal: national legislation. 'Social regeneration through legislative catharsis', as John Bowen put it (2006: 16), capturing the essence of the 2004 anti-headscarf law.

France's master thinker, Pierre Bourdieu, who showed himself otherwise uninterested in his country's protracted *affaires de foulard*, surmised that 'the patent question of whether "Islamic" headscarves should be accepted in schools masks the latent question of whether immigrants of North African origin should be accepted in France' (quoted in Laurence and Vaisse 2006: 163). The sociologist's professional unmasking overlooks the enormous provocation that Islam must constitute to republican self-definition. Both clash head-on in that Islam pushes the private into the public sphere by not recognizing this distinction, while republicanism has an expansive definition of 'public' which in turn 'desiccate[s . . .] the private sphere' (Levinson 1997: 356). If Islam sternly denies the very distinction private–public, which is the essence of republicanism, how could one ever expect the two systems to coexist peacefully? Surely the word is one thing, the lived reality quite another. But in philosophical France the word is no empty shell, and this, incidentally, is something it shares with 'scriptural' Islam.

Bourdieu's knee-jerking charge of discrimination and exclusion also obscures the fact that Muslim integration in France has been stunningly successful, at least in socio-cultural terms.[2] Despite the state's heavy hand on the headscarf, a recent survey found 42 percent of the Muslims in France considering themselves 'French first, Muslim second'. Note that only seven percent of British Muslims, despite (or perhaps because of) being pampered by 'multiculturalism', rank allegiance to their country above allegiance to their religion (Schain 2007: 46, table 6). Further, a greater percentage of French Muslims than of French Christians think that democracy in France works well – almost 70 percent of Muslims, but only 63 percent of Protestants and 58 percent of Catholics think so (Laurence and Vaisse 2006: 47). Such views are reciprocated (should one say: rewarded?) by ordinary French people, 74 percent of whom think that there is no conflict between 'being a devout Muslim' and 'living in a modern society' (Pew Research Center 2006: 3). Rather than being a smokescreen for exclusion, 'republican' integration sets very clear and firm rules; but the message tends to be heard, and those who abide by it are in turn invited to the 'dining-table of the republic'.[3]

This is more than the high-flying rhetoric of ministers of internal affairs. Any discussion of Islam in France must start from the fact of a high degree of acculturation, even secularism, among French Muslims (a phenomenon first revealed by Tribalat 1995). Almost 80 percent of French Muslims feel 'comfortable with people of different religions dating or marrying' (Laurence and Vaisse 2006: 43). The intermarriage rate in France is the highest among European Muslims: half of French male Muslims marry non-Muslim women and one fourth of Muslim females marry non-Muslim men, thus breaking a key taboo in Islam. 61 percent of French Muslims say they have 'many' French non-Muslim friends (ibid.). On the religious side, almost 70 percent of French Muslims support *laïcité* (henceforth also referred to by the English word 'laicity'), that is, the strict separation between church and state (Giry 2006: 4). In fact, only 8 to 15 percent of French

Muslims regularly attend religious services and less than 5 percent attend the mosque each Friday (Laurence and Vaisse 2006: 76). Interestingly, recent immigrants from sub-Saharan Africa are the most observant of ritual, while the classic post-colonial immigrants from Algeria are the least (ibid. 87). One is usually impressed by the estimated figure of 5 million Muslims residing in France, which makes them by far the largest Muslim minority in Europe: one third of the European total. But their overwhelming majority is Muslim only in ethnic, not in religious terms. In France, 'Islam' is an issue for only a minority within a minority.

On the opposite side, one must realize that the republicanism that has framed the reception of Islam and of Muslims in France is a variant of liberalism. In fact, French republicanism strikingly resembles 'political liberalism' (Rawls 1993). Both share an iron-clad distinction between public and private, and especially a demanding abstraction from merely private concerns and idioms in the public sphere. As Rawls reminds us in the opening pages of his *Political Liberalism*, the historical origin of liberalism is in the privatization of religion, which in France is referred to as *laïcité*. While in the private sphere one may be a religious believer, in the public sphere one becomes a citizen engaged in 'public reasoning' (Rawls 1993: 212ff), abstracted from one's private demons. One never uses religious or other 'comprehensive doctrines' there, but only a political (read: republican) language which may be understood and agreed upon by those who are otherwise divided by religion or ideology. As Cécile Laborde observes, 'French republicanism is a tough-minded version of egalitarian, difference-blind liberalism' (Laborde 2005: 315).

'Tough-minded' indeed – and here the parallel with political liberalism ends. Because what Rawls construed as bottom-up agreement among free, if 'reasonable', people who are adhering to many creeds and ways of life has in France been the top-down result of a 'strong formative project' undertaken by the state (Laborde 2005: 316). This is where a decidedly non-Anglo-Saxon component kicks in. As John Bowen (2006: 15) put it concisely, it is, at heart, Rousseau versus Locke – 'freedom through the state' versus 'freedom from the state'. French liberalism is distinguished from the more pragmatic-minded Anglo-Saxon variant by being an ethical project of the state. Both are one-sided incarnations of a tension, inherent in liberalism, between its being either a substantive way of life or a procedure for reconciling many ways of life (Gray 2000). Situated within a long tradition of state-centered society-building which reaches back to the late medieval period (see Strayer 1970), French liberalism is a distinctly ethical, society-building project.

Symptomatic of this is a long-standing obsession with 'integration' in French intellectual discourse. Long before the notion of integration came to target immigrants, French classic sociology, and the work of Emile Durkheim above all, was driven by the question of what it is that integrates an entire society – especially a modern, differentiated, and individualized society, where everything and everyone flees the center. There is always an assumption that integration does not just happen, as tends to be the view across the Channel, but must be the work of an art – be it that of 'religion' in a monarchic age, or of 'politics' in a democratic age (see Schnapper 1994). In this perspective, laicity is not just the French way of privatizing religion, but also an 'essential attribute of the modern state' which 'transcends the diversity of religious beliefs', symbolizing that 'the social tie is no longer religious but national and thus political' (ibid., pp. 73f). Integration, be it through religion or through politics, implies a 'transcendence', an abstracting from one's particular allegiances and origin features. No wonder that the transcendent takes on the air of the sacred, which in the democratic age simply becomes transferred from religion to the nation. One can see: the axiomatic assumption of the 'state's transformative role' (Bowen 2006: 15) threatens to transform liberalism into something else. Friedrich Hayek, in one of the central texts of twentieth-century liberalism, even thinks that 'Gallican' liberty, with its penchant for the 'speculative and rationalistic', foreshadows the very destruction of liberalism by ' "social" and totalitarian democracy' (Hayek 1960: 55).

One also sees, again, how much Islam must be an affront to republican liberalism, because of the latter's 'expansive' definition of the public as space to be cleansed from religion and ethnicity and to be filled in by universalistic values and commitments. Especially Islam's refusal to separate spiritual from temporal spheres raises suspicion. As Dominique Schnapper flatly states, because Islam is 'at the same time a religion and a political system', it 'contradicts the requirements of the French state' (quoted in Laborde 2005: 320). Interestingly, this view is confirmed, on the side of Islam, by the leading Muslim jurist Yusuf al-Qaradawi, who finds that 'from the Islamic point of view, everything pertains to religion, and everything pertains to the law' (ibid.). Competing scopes make for competing allegiances: the universalistic scope of Islam clashes with the French priority accorded to national citizenship. In a recent British government project to placate recalcitrant Muslims, one finds the strange concept of a 'British Muslim citizenship', which places commitments to the 'world' and to the 'umma' ahead of a commitment to 'Britain' proper. This would have caused a national alert in France. Note that hell broke loose when a French Muslim leader stated that 'the Koran is our constitution' (quoted and discussed in Bowen 2007a: 1008).

But all this would perhaps not matter much if the values propagated by Islam matched those of the republic. This is why gender equality becomes a central element in the French encounter with Islam. At a recent Franco-German summit discussing immigrant integration, the German chancellor reportedly emphasized the importance of language acquisition, while the French president talked mostly about the rights of women.[4] Indeed, the headscarf's being oppressive of women was a (perhaps the) main reason for legislating against it in 2004. As Prime Minister Raffarin put it before the National Assembly: 'For me, there is one criterion in favor of the (headscarf) law [. . . It] will be good if it protects women, all women; that is the key point. This will be the first of the criteria of the law [. . .] that we propose' (quoted in Gresh 2004: 270). However, sacking the headscarf for the sake of republican equality required violating another republican value: liberty. More concretely, prohibiting the headscarf required an objective reading of the meaning of the headscarf on the part of the state and a disregard for the multiplicity of subjective meanings of the headscarf which, as the Conseil d'Etat had established in its case decisions, could be deciphered only case by case.

Next to collision, however, there has also been collusion between the French state and Islam, in prolongation of the 'Gallican Church' tradition of 'control of religion by the state through selective recognition and support of religious institutions' (Bowen 2007a: 1008). Echoing the late medieval creation of a Gallican Church that was to be independent of Rome, the past two decades were marked by state attempts to transform Islam, from being 'in France', to being 'of France', and to appoint a Muslim chief as the central interlocutor of the state – much as there were already Catholic, Protestant, and Jewish chiefs around. This process, crowned by the creation of the Conseil Français du Culte Musulman (CFCM) under the then Minister of the Interior Nicolas Sarkozy in 2003, has pushed the French state into a kind of de facto multiculturalism which contradicts its republican ideology. One observer even characterized the recognition of the quintessentially multicultural 'principle of compensation' as the 'official position of the Minister of the Interior' (Basdevant-Gaudemet 2000: 107, 103). According to this view, the French state owes Islam preferential treatment, in order to rectify the latter's many disadvantages vis-à-vis the historically established religions, especially (but not exclusively) with respect to the licensing and financing of prayer spaces.[5] In the always subversive view of Nicolas Sarkozy, state-supported religion could even take the place of exhausted republicanism: 'Today our neighborhoods are spiritual deserts [. . .] I don't say that the Republic cannot [. . .] speak to young people about self-respect and respect for others and for women [. . .]. But [. . .] the Republic is not up to the task and doesn't do it. It is in this sense that religions are a benefit for the Republic. Religions give today's men and women the perspective of fundamental questions of human existence: the meaning of life and death and society and history' (quoted in Schain 2007: 15).

Overall, the relationship between Gallicanism and republicanism has been one of dialectical tension. Not by accident, the inauguration of the Conseil Français du Culte Musulman in May 2003 was *also* the galvanizing moment of the anti-headscarf law, which was passed one year later. After being booed from stage at the annual convention of the powerful Union of French Islamic Organizations (UOIF) for insisting that 'republican' law required unveiled heads on ID cards, Sarkozy drew the connection: 'I had to come here. This is the counterpart to organizing the (Muslim) cult.'[6] On this view, the reaffirmation of republican principles with the 2004 anti-headscarf law was a compensation for having gone (too) far in recognizing Islam within the Gallic Church framework – especially by cow-towing to the radical UOIF, which traces its roots to the Egyptian fundamentalist Muslim Brotherhood.

But the matter is more complicated still. As I will spell out in the remainder of this chapter, the republican principle of *laïcité* that stood to be reinvigorated in the anti-headscarf law is no monolithic thing. Instead, it is marked by a tension between being a principle of rights and religious liberties *and* being a principle of national unity and integration: both the defense *and* the rejection of the Islamic headscarf could be done (and historically have been done) in the name of *laïcité*. France's highest administrative court, the Conseil d'Etat, took laicity to be a principle of rights; political state actors, by contrast, took it to be a principle of unity. The 2004 anti-headscarf law is, then, a vindication of the political over the legal branches of the state, political backlash against rights-oriented courts in the context of a globally politicized Islam, which was seen as putting to the test the republican institution par excellence: the public school.

The Two Forms of Laicity: Rights versus Unity

In March 2004, with the overwhelming support of the political right and left, the French national assembly passed a law prohibiting pupils from wearing or displaying 'ostensible' religious signs in public schools. It essentially consists of a single sentence: 'In public schools the carrying of signs or dress through which students ostensibly manifest a religious belonging is prohibited.' In its caustic brevity, the law concludes fifteen years of protracted struggle surrounding the Islamic headscarf in French public schools.

The *laïcité* that is meant to be reinforced by the 2004 law has always been marked by a tension between individual rights and statist unity. This tension is inherent in the first two articles of the 1905 Law on the Separation between Church and State, the legal cornerstone of French *laïcité* (curiously, that text does not mention the word)[7]. Article 1 of the 1905 law enshrines the principle of religious liberty: 'The republic assures the freedom of conscience.' By contrast, Article 2 stipulates the republic-defining separation between state and church: 'The republic does not recognize, nor remunerate or support any cult.' Notionally a principle of non-intervention, Article 2 has since been creatively reinterpreted in two activist directions. *Either* it is taken to denote a positive intervention in support of religion – but one that has to be even-handed or equalizing. As the chief of the Ministry of Interior's religious bureau put it, the meaning of Article 2 is that 'the Republic does not decide to favour one religion or to favour one school of thought within a religion' (quoted in Bowen 2007b: 11). *Or* it is taken to denote a negative type of intervention, with the purpose of silencing assertive religion when this 'is really necessary for order and social cohesion' (Messner et al. 2003: 49).

Overall, however, the law of 1905 is cut from a liberal cloth, with a reconciliation-minded Aristide Briand prevailing over the militant anti-clericalism of Emile Combes: rather than being geared toward destroying organized religions root-and-branch, as had been the purpose of the 1901 Law on Associations (which required a legislative approval for religious associations which was denied en bloc), the 1905 law guaranteed their continued existence, if only with the diminished status of private organizations. Still, a conflict between laicity understood as religious liberty and laicity understood as republican self-definition was always possible on the grounds of the 1905 law. After all, its passing was enough of an affront for the Vatican to break diplomatic relations with France for some twenty years.

With respect to the two faces of laicity, a distinction is generally made between a 'combative' and a 'pluralist' laicity (among many, Fetzer and Soper 2005: 73–6), the first being in favor of republican unity, the second defending religious rights. The interesting matter is that, when the conflict over the Islamic headscarf first erupted in the late 1980s, liberal laicity seemed to have won the upper hand over republican laicity.[8] Pierre Birnbaum (2001, ch. 6) even spoke of a 'retreat from the republican state' and of a 'Protestantization of French society' in which the values of individualism, tolerance, and secularism had become dominant, the 'state reach[ing] out to the Church' and political leaders from de Gaulle to Mitterand and Chirac displaying in public their Catholic faith, without many qualms. The logic of this evolution is clear: once the Catholic Church no longer represented a serious challenge to the republican state, the latter could accept its presence and even harness its positive function in society. J. M. Woehrling (1998) spoke in this respect of a transformation from a 'negative' into a 'positive' notion of state neutrality: the first predominated in the 1905 law, in which the state refused to have anything to do with religion, while the second has become dominant today, when the state has relaxed enough to acknowledge the social utility of religion.

A noted sociologist of religion characterized the evolution of laicity from combat to pluralism in terms of a 'laïcisation de la laïcité': 'Laïcité defines itself more like a regulatory framework for a pluralism of world views than like a counter-system to religion' (Willaime 1998: 15). This view had first been laid out by jurist Jean Rivero, who described the transformation of laicity from 'ideology' into 'legal rule' (Rivero 1960), so that in the end 'laicity implies no longer a uniformity of thinking and of doctrine but a consensus on pluralism' (Messner et al. 2003: 124).

On this view, the old 'laicity of combat' had shared with its Catholic opponent a mystification and an idolatry towards institutions, which were in both cases endowed with sacred value. Had not the men of 1789 replaced the *ancien régime* with their own 'civic religion' and sacred institutions? As David Martin observed in his classic *A General Theory of Secularization* (1978: 24), 'the nexus of French Enlightenment doctrines resembles a Catholicism inverted and the secular religions produced by France are sometimes a form of Catholicism without Christianity'.There has been a continuation of the idea that the state is engaged in an ethical project of producing virtuous citizens in a good society. As Jean Baubérot expressed it (1990: 139): 'To the notion of the Catholic Church as mediator has corresponded the belief of the revolutionaries in the all-powerfulness of institutions for the good [*bonheur*] of human-beings.' French republican nation-builders, past and present, are practising Durkheimians according to whom the 'sacred' and the 'profane' is a universal dichotomy of society and integration and unity rest on shielding an intangible, foundational realm of the sacred from the reaches of profanity (see also Shils 1972). In this '*catho-laïcité*' (E. Morin 1990), the Christian Holy Trinity has simply been replaced by 'the providential trinity Reason–Science–Progress' (p. 38). That this line of thought is not dead is demonstrated by the sacralization of the public school in contemporary republican discourse. Note how Nicolas Sarkozy, arguably the least republican among today's French political elite, spelled out the terms of 'inviting Islam to the dining-table of the republic': 'If I enter a mosque I take off my shoes. If a young Muslim enters school, she has to take off her veil.'[9]

To the degree that laicity itself is being laicized and thus transformed from one 'of combat' into one 'of pluralism', the republican institutions are stripped of their sacred aura and the right of the individual takes primacy. Jean Baubérot (2004: 67) spoke in this respect of 'a new anticlericalism, this time with regard to secular institutions and their clerks'. Just when the forces of individualism were inevitably corroding the 'traditional catholic conception of institution' (p. 145), which the republicans had simply adopted and refashioned in their own secular way, the famous Foulard Affair of 1989 erupted. It reinvigorated what had been considered dead by then – the '*laïcité du combat*'. Note that this phrase was approvingly adopted in the Foulard Affair's notorious opening salvo, the open letter to Prime Minister Lionel Jospin, 'Teachers, don't capitulate', signed by five 'republican' intellectuals:

> Laicity has always been a relation between forces [*un rapport de forces*]. Now that the religions have again acquired an appetite for combat, is it the right moment to abandon what is commonly called the 'laicity of combat' for the sake of good manners? Laicity is and remains in principle a struggle, much like the public school, the republic, and liberty itself. Their survival requires from all of us discipline, sacrifices, and a bit of courage.[10]

Jospin's initial reaction to the refusal of three Muslim girls to take off their veil in a public school in Creil, a *banlieue* of Paris, had showed a preference for 'dialogue' and for accommodating the veil in the interest of the pupil: 'The school must not exclude because its purpose is inclusion [*elle est faite pour accueillir*]' (quoted in Gaspard and Khosrokhavar 1995: 22). The republican intellectuals, including Alain Finkielkraut, Elisabeth Badinter, and Régis Debray, gunned down this not unreasonable stance as 'Munich of the republican school', associating the lax approach to Islam with the infamous 'appeasement' policy of France and Britain toward Nazi Germany in 1938.[11] Interestingly, the 'laicity of combat' which stood to be reinvigorated in this polemic was not so much directed against the incriminated religious behavior itself as against its wrongheaded toleration by a lax 'new laicity'[12]. In other words, this time round it was not so much a conflict between the forces of laicity, on the one side, and the forces of religion, on the other, as in the nineteenth-century battle of the republican state against the Catholic Church; rather, it was now a conflict between two different understandings of laicity, which, in principle, was shared and consented to by all, but in reality was given two opposite meanings: liberal versus republican.

The Conseil d'Etat and Liberal Laicity

As the liberal version of laicity centers on rights of the individual, it is no wonder that the judiciary has been its key agent within the state – and with considerable success – long before the confrontation with Islam (see Rivero 1960). Court-driven, liberal laicity continued to be dominant between the Foulard Affair in 1989 and the Law on Laicity in 2004. While the Foulard Affair was everywhere taken as a sign of the archaic illiberalism of the republican French state, few non-French observers took notice that it was resolved in favor of the Muslim girls and that recurrent episodes of expulsion of veiled students by school directors almost always ended with the students' court-ordered readmission. Of 49 contested expulsions that were considered by the Conseil d'Etat, between 1992 and 1999, 41 cases were revoked by court order (Haut Conseil à l'intégration 2000: 56).

The key for installing liberal laicity toward Islam was the Conseil d'Etat's influential *avis* (advice) of 27 November 1989, which came to define the legal status quo with respect to the Muslim headscarf for the next fifteen years. Annulling the famous exclusion of three Muslim girls from a school in Creil, the court argued that laicity meant different things for teachers and students: for teachers it meant 'neutrality', that is, abstaining from identifying with, or inculcating, a creed; for students it meant the 'freedom of conscience', which allowed them to express their religious affiliation in public schools. The court formulated this two-pronged approach to laicity: 'the principle of laicity requires that instruction occurs in respect of neutrality on the part of teachers, and in respect of the freedom of conscience on the part of students' (the *avis* is reprinted in William 1991). Accordingly, as donning a headscarf was an expression of fundamental religious liberties, protected by constitutional texts and by international conventions that France had signed, the toleration of the headscarf in public schools was always the rule, while its prohibition was at best the exception that had to be determined case by case.

This does not mean that there were no limits to toleration. Such limits consisted, first, of an absolute obligation of students to attend all courses of study. The strict handling of this obligation in subsequent court decisions distinguishes the French from other continental legal approaches on this matter (for the latter, see Albers 1994). Secondly and more relevantly for the handling of the headscarf itself, a limit to toleration was reached in cases of an 'ostentatious' carrying of the veil which amounted to acts of 'pressure, provocation, proselytism or propaganda', and which violated the rights of other 'members of the educational community' or endangered the orderly functioning of the school. One could say: as a religious symbol, the headscarf was 'in'; as a political symbol, it was 'out'. Unfortunately, especially in the age of a globally politicized Islam, this was a distinction rife with ambiguity, and perhaps one that, in principle, is impossible to draw (see Chapter 5).

However, the 1989 *avis* did little more than summarize past jurisdiction; and it was not legally binding. The first hard legal intervention of the Conseil d'Etat occurred only three years later, in the so-called *l'affaire Montfermeil*. It concerned three Muslim girls who had been expelled by a *collège* (middle school) in Montfermeil near Paris, on the basis of an internal school order which flatly 'prohibited' the Muslim headscarf (like 'all religious, political or philosophical signs') and thus directly negated the case-by-case approach stipulated by the Conseil d'Etat in 1989. In an *arrêt* on 2 November 1992,[13] the Conseil d'Etat declared this prohibition 'illegal' because of the 'generality of [its] terms', and the girls were readmitted by order. This was a deeply ironic ruling, as a local case-by-case approach was ordered top-down, above the heads of local school authorities, and it has drawn the ire of headscarf foes and of the critics of an overly 'liberal' Conseil d'Etat ever since (see the furious critique by Coq 2003, ch. 6).

What became known as the Conseil d'Etat's 'Kherouaa decision' is important in a second respect also, as it brought to the fore the different semiotics deployed by headscarf friends and foes. If one tolerated the headscarf, it was on the basis of a subjective approach that left its interpretation to the woman wearing it; if one opposed it, this was on the basis of an objective approach where the meaning of the headscarf could be established by the state. The case for the subjective approach, which came to be adopted by the Conseil d'Etat, was laid out by the court's *maître de requêtes* in the Kherouaa case, David Kessler (Kessler 1993). And, acidly attacked by Guy Coq (2003:

ch. 6), this was a dubious case which raises the question: if the swastika is prohibited (as it is, under French anti-discrimination law), why tolerate the headscarf? Kessler argued that, in the swastika, 'the sign itself', irrespective of any 'interpretation', constituted 'a provocation to hatred' (p. 117). By contrast, with respect to the headscarf, 'not the sign itself but its perception' mattered, and 'interpreting the place of this sign within Islam' on the part of administration or judge would 'seriously violate the principles of the laic state, of religious liberty, and of the respect for the freedom of conscience' (ibid.). This was the position taken by courts outside France as well. However, it was inconsistent, as Coq (2003, ch. 6) pointed out with great aplomb. The distinction between 'sign itself' and signs that require 'interpretation' is impossible to draw: all signs require interpretation, the swastika included. And to classify the headscarf as religious symbol – which is required in order to bring it within the ambit of constitutional liberty rights – is, of course, an act of 'interpretation'. But then, why not interpret the headscarf as symbol of sexism, as its foes do? One sees that the semiotic agnosticism on which toleration of the headscarf rests is inconsistent; but, conversely, with what assurance can the headscarf foes claim to establish its objective meaning, without a margin of inherently subjective 'interpretation'? The unavoidable semiotics of the headscarf is treacherous ground for headscarf friends and foes alike.

Having said this, the Conseil d'Etat's liberal, rights-centered version of laicity became the dominant approach toward Islam. The Haut Conseil à l'intégration (2000) came to share it, too. In its report *L'Islam dans la république*, the Haut Conseil presented the law of 1905 as 'above all a law of liberty', protective of the individual and collective liberties of religious worship, even in public, and securing the equality of all religions; only secondarily was it a republican 'law of separation' (p. 14). As two furious dissidents of the Haut Conseil pointed out (Kaltenbach and Tribalat 2002: 212), the Conseil d'Etat's strong interpretation of religious liberties, which included the students' 'right to express and manifest their religious beliefs *within the school establishment*',[14] crossed out the principle of neutrality as understood from a republican perspective. This was because the public school was now bound to transmute from republican 'sanctuary' into a mirror, or even amplifier, of the ethnic and religious diversity of society (ibid.).

To the degree that laicity had classically been associated with republican neutrality – that is, has been regarded as one where the strictures of public homogeneity expansively intruded into the private sphere – one scholar even stated that 'religious liberty now appears as a value superior to laicity' (Barbier 1993: 84). The identification of laicity with a certain, republican understanding of neutrality, and its juxtaposition with an extraneously conceived principle of religious liberties, can often be found in the French debate surrounding the Islamic headscarf. This is misleading because, enshrined as it is in the first article of the 1905 Law on the Separation of Church and State, the protection of religious liberties is part and parcel of the laic tradition itself.

An equally important reference point for liberal laicity is Jules Ferry's famous *Lettre aux instituteurs* (1883), which had pioneered the two-pronged approach to laicity later adopted by the Conseil d'Etat. According to Ferry, teachers, not students, were the principal addressees of laicity's neutrality mandate. They were asked to abstain from anything that could violate or offend the religious sentiments of students, and thus to respect laicity's mandate of religious liberty. The most famous passage of Ferry's letter is the following: 'Ask yourselves whether only one family father, present in your class and listening to you, could in good faith refuse his assent to what you say. If the answer is yes, abstain from saying what you intended to say [. . .] One cannot pay too much attention when touching on something as delicate and sacred as a child's conscience.' Certainly, this liberal abstention was then justified, in classically republican terms, by the euphoric assumption that what was communicated in public school was not just 'personal wisdom', but 'human wisdom' of a 'universal order' that belonged to the 'patrimony of humanity' (ibid.).

While a liberal streak has been evidently part of the laic tradition from the start, the Conseil d'Etat's emphasis on rights was *also* in line with the general legal evolution, in the wake of which power-wielding institutions have been infused with a discourse of rights which is protective of those subjected to them. As Conseil d'Etat member David Kessler (1993) holds in his opinion on the Kherouaa case, 'I don't think that German or English courts would have decided differently' (101). In fact, Article 10 of the 1989 Law on Education, approvingly cited in the 1989 *avis* of the Conseil d'Etat, stipulates: 'The pupils, within the confines of pluralism and of the principle of neutrality, dispose of liberty of information and liberty of expression' (quoted in Gresh 2004: 293). Dominique Schnapper (2006), an ardent republican sociologist, has diagnosed the underlying development as the inevitable 'loss of transcendence' of the contemporary nation–state.

Sensing that the winds of change were of a global nature, critics of liberal laicity were consequently boxed into the position that laicity, properly understood, was 'a French exception' (Debray 1990), to be retained for its own sake. Key to this was to stress the centrality of the public school for republican nation-building. For Régis Debray, 'laicity is the possibility to lead a double life, from one's childhood on', with the school as a 'separate space [. . .] where the particularisms and factual conditions [of life] are suspended' (ibid., pp. 200f). The public school allowed the child to emancipate herself from the confines of her social background and to become a true *citoyenne*. Only if one holds it against this republican ideal does one understand the enormous provocation inherent in Pierre Bourdieu and Jean-Claude Passeron's famous claim about the school-based 'reproduction' of class inequality (1970). But such emancipation required strict dualistic dichotomies between 'home' and 'school', 'private' and 'public', 'civil society' and 'public space'. In furthering emancipation, the school realized a key value of republicanism. This made it 'sacred', because – as the Durkheimian Debray knows – 'what makes for the unity of a social group is considered by it to be sacred' (Debray 1990: 205). From this angle, the liberal idea of 'laicizing laicity' amounted to a 'reclericalizing the social' as source of poisonous diversity; and, instead of 'redefining' laicity, the need was to 'bring it back to life' (ibid.).

All the attacks on the headscarf, from 1989 on, were premised on a sacralization of the school. In 'Profs, don't capitulate', the school was 'the only institution that is devoted to the universal', while 'communitarian pressures' threatened to reduce it to a 'school of social predestination'.[15] The Bayrou *décret* of 1994 – the first direct political attack on the liberal Conseil d'Etat, which mandated the generic suppression of 'ostentatious' religious signs in school – was a lyrical resurrection of the republican, nation-building school:

> The nation is not only an ensemble of rights-holding citizens. It is a community of destiny. This ideal is constructed above all in the school. The school is the site *par excellence* of education and integration, where all the children find themselves learning to live together and to respect one another [. . .] All discrimination, sexual, cultural, or religious, must stop at the school gates. This laic and national ideal is the substance of the republican school and the foundation of its mandate of civic education.[16]

The Stasi Report (2003), which laid the grounds for the 2004 anti-headscarf law, blew the same horn: 'The school is a fundamental institution of the republic' teaching minors to 'live together beyond their differences', which required protecting them 'from the furor of the world' (p. 56). In turn, with an eye on the desacralization of the school in contemporary rights discourse, the 'republican school assembles not simple users (of institutions) but pupils who are destined to become enlightened citizens' (ibid.).

Implicit in the Conseil d'Etat's 'laicity at variable geometry' (Kaltenbach and Tribalat 2002: 119) is indeed a denial of the special status of the public school for the republican project. Rather, liberal laicity rests on a distinction between the 'providers' and the 'users' of services within indistinct state institutions, be they the post office or the school, and different aspects of laicity are then held to apply on each side ('neutrality' for providers, 'liberty' for users). The notorious 'Dr Abdallah', popularizing the Conseil d'Etat jurisdiction for the Muslim grassroots, put it this way: 'The neutrality of public service, whether it is that of the Post or that of the School, imposes itself on the provider of this service, and not on its user.'[17] This view is confirmed in the authoritative *Traité de droit français des religions* (Messner et al. 2003), according to which the 'neutrality' of the public school only extends to the teachers, the programs, the building, and the site, but *not* to the pupils' (p. 1119). Against it, Kaltenbach and Tribalat (2002) pointed out that the Law on Education of 10 July 1989, which had been passed just a few months before the Conseil d'Etat's landmark *avis* on the Creil exclusions, *also* contained the holistic notion of an 'educational community' which engaged both the teachers and the students in a joint educational project and defied the provider/user dualism that might make sense for more mundane institutions, such as the post office. Article 10 of the 1989 Law on Education, usually taken as a religious liberty clause, might then be taken as extending the neutrality principle to the students and deriving from this a restriction of their religious expressions: 'In the schools [*collèges*] [. . .] students enjoy liberty of information [. . .] and expression, *within the limits of respecting* [. . .] *the principle of neutrality*' (quoted ibid., p. 121; emphasis added). This is the road *not* taken by the Conseil d'Etat in its decisions in the following years; conversely, it is the road taken by the 2004 Law on Laicity. The Debré Rapport, commissioned by the National Assembly in competition with the Presidential Stasi Commission, promptly invoked the formula of an 'educational community' different from the social relationships in ordinary public institutions: 'Students are not simple users of public services but individuals in the making within an institution whose mission is to form them' (Debré Rapport 2003, tome 1, 1ère partie, p. 30).

Despite the liberal jurisdiction of the Conseil d'Etat, which generally *accepted* the veil as an expression of religious liberties, local school directors were still held, by government decree, to enter into a 'dialogue' with students, the single purpose of which was the *removal* of the veil. This inconsistency had existed since the first Jospin *décret* which followed upon, and implemented, the *avis* of the Conseil d'Etat in November 1989: 'One immediately must engage in a dialogue with the student and her parents, so that she renounces to carry religious signs, in the interest of the student and of a good functioning of the school.'[18]

Pressed by local school administrators for clearer and more objective guidelines as to when religious symbols were to be prohibited, the government responded with the so-called Bayrou *décret* of 1994 (issued by Minister of Education François Bayrou). The decree introduced a distinction between 'discrete' signs, which 'express a personal attachment to [someone's] convictions', and 'ostentatious signs, which constitute *in themselves* elements of proselytism or of discrimination' (emphasis added).[19] Issued for the sake of clarity and objectivity, the Bayrou *décret* squarely contradicted the Conseil d'Etat's *démarche* on the veil: if the latter had declared that the veil itself was not prohibited, but only its 'ostentatious port', the Bayrou *décret* turned this around, declaring certain signs to be illicit 'in themselves'. However, this obvious obstruction of the Conseil d'Etat remained without practical consequence. The Conseil d'Etat took it as a mere 'interpretation' of the law and proceeded with its traditionally liberal line.

Accordingly, the legal status quo preceding the 2004 Law on Laicity was this: the Conseil d'Etat's liberal approach to laicity conditioned a general toleration of the Muslim veil, whereas the more restrictive circulars of various ministers of education had the subordinate status of mere 'interpretations' of the law and thus were without real effect. Overall there was no legislative basis for prohibiting the veil, which the state still prescribed in its circulars, from Jospin to Bayrou. But European human rights norms required that restrictions of the exercise of a fundamental freedom needed a statutory legal basis. This is how the so-called Debré Commission, established by the French Assemblée Nationale in the summer of 2003 to advise on the veil, justified its recommendation for a law on laicity in December 2003 (Debré Rapport 2003, tome 1, p. 33).

The Victory of Republican Laicity in the Political Sphere

The road to the 2004 Law on Laicity may be summarized as the 'triumph of a political enterprise' (Lorcerie 2005: 11), or simply as a 'politicians' takeover' (Bowen 2006: 98–112). The opening shot is generally taken to be the tumultuous (though acidly calculated) appearance of the then Minister of the Interior Nicolas Sarkozy at the annual meeting of France's major Muslim organization, *Union des Organisations Islamiques de France* (UOIF), on 19 April 2003, near Paris. When Sarkozy suddenly switched from the expected back-patting to advising the Muslim audience that pictures on ID cards had to be taken with heads uncovered because this was required by 'republican law',[20] the audience was up on its feet and the rest of his speech was drowned in boos and hisses. The media immediately picked up the issue and would not let it down until a headscarf law was passed eleven months later.[21] Sarkozy, who, ironically, turned out to be the sole opponent to a ban on the headscarf within the French political elite, later characterized his 19 April intervention as 'my reply to April 21st' (ibid. 102) – that traumatic spring Sunday of 2002, when Le Pen had ousted Socialist front-runner Lionel Jospin in the first round of the presidential election. On that day too, President Chirac was reborn as a republican savior with the perceived mission to maintain national cohesion above party lines.[22] A law on laicity was tailor-made for that cause.

Accordingly, one will not find a dramatic grassroots event similar to the 1989 Foulard Affair, nor will one find an alarming rise in the number of veiled students to trigger the law. In fact, the number of concrete conflicts surrounding the veil was at a ten-year low in the summer of 2003.[23] At the opening of the school year in September 2003 there were 1,256 counted cases of veiled students throughout France. This was only slightly above the 1,123 cases counted in 1994, the year of the Bayrou *décret* and a moment of high tension. Moreover, three months later, in December 2003, there remained only twenty unresolved cases, and only four of them ended in a forced exclusion. In a total school-student population of 9 million, these are exceedingly small numbers. Nicolas Sarkozy, who produced these numbers before the Debré Commission, was right: 'But to say that the Republic is in danger, considering these figures, is a stupidity' (Debré Rapport 2003, tome II, 6ème partie, p. 112). Moreover, only 5 percent of all French schools – namely those in the depressed *banlieues* with a disproportionate concentration of Muslim ethnics – were affected by the phenomenon of headscarf-wearing pupils at all (ibid., tome 1, 1ère partie, p. 51). Finally, if one considers that less than 12 percent of all the French Muslims are currently taken to be practising their religion (p. 67), one cannot conclude that social reality itself created the need for a corrective anti-headscarf law. Accordingly the Debré Commission was forced to concede the following: 'Communitarian claims-making actually does not reflect any sociological reality whatsoever in France and it has to be seen more as political agitation by a small number of individuals' (p. 68). It is telling that the parallel Stasi Commission spoke of a 'permanent *guerilla* war against laicity' (Stasi Report 2003, section 3. 2. 2., emphasis added). A 'guerilla', after all, is something one cannot openly see.

The one constant element in the French state's dealing with Islam, however, was a deep fear of violence. This fear perennially colored the perception of the Islamic headscarf in terms of an equation 'headscarf = Islam = terrorism' (Bowen 2006: 90). Ever since the traumatic Algerian war of independence, there was the (not unfounded) suspicion that postcolonial immigrants from these quarters harbored hostile feelings toward the French state. Since 1989, the year of the first head-scarf controversy, there was a bloody civil war in Algeria between its military government and a militant Islamic movement, and it threatened to spill over to France because of the French government's backing of the Algerian government. 1995 saw the lethal bombing of the Paris Métro by Islamic militants, and French police forces ended the life of fiery *banlieue* terrorist Khaled Kelkal. In the early 2000s, the second Intifada in Palestine and global terrorism were feared to find ample resonance in the depressed *banlieues*. Nicolas Sarkozy's frantic push for a representative Muslim organization (CFCM) has to be seen in this context. As he urged French Muslim leaders in the winter of 2003, 'you must finish creating the CFCM [. . .] quickly in order to respond to any violence that might destabilize French society and discredit the Muslim community by throwing it and the Jewish community into opposition' (quoted by Laurence and Vaisse 2006: 157f). In fact, since not just the largest Muslim but also the largest Jewish community in Europe called France their home, the Middle Eastern and global conflicts surrounding Islam threatened to translate into domestic conflicts. Note that, when cross-party support for an anti-headscarf law was building up in 2003, the book of the day was *Les Territoires perdues de la république* (Brenner 2002), which claimed that 'Shoah cannot be taught' in the schools of the *banlieues* on account of Islamic militancy.

Against the growing specter of violence, liberal laicity was a luxury that could no longer be afforded. As the Stasi Commission (2003: 58) put it laconically, 'today the question is no longer the freedom of conscience but public order'. Its final report drew an almost paranoid picture of 'organized groups testing the resistance of the republic' (p. 43).[24] The reflections of its single dissenting member, the noted sociologist of laicity Jean Baubérot, offer some insight into the pressures and the group-think which led even those members of the commission who initially had been against a law to end up in favor of one. According to Baubérot (2005), a few emotionally charged testimonies from harassed Muslim women created the impression of an 'Islamic threat', even though no concrete social-scientific evidence existed, so that the representative nature of these testimonies could not be corroborated. In fact, not to have commissioned its own survey of the headscarf reality, and not to review at least the evidence available from French sociology about the frequency and the motivations of wearing the headscarf, are among the most striking omissions of the Stasi Commission. This is all the more astonishing if one considers that in no other country of the world have the actual motivations for wearing a headscarf been more thoroughly studied. With only one exception at the very end, no veil-wearing Muslim woman was invited to testify before the commission.

In the insider's view of the Stasi Commission offered by Baubérot, the issue of women's rights became 'a dominant idea', turning around initially unenthusiastic members in favor of a law against the headscarf. A case in point is that of immigration expert Patrick Weil. He professedly had entered the commission being predisposed against such a law, but he left being in favor of it, the reason being that 'wearing the scarf or imposing it upon others has become an issue not of individual freedom but of a national strategy of fundamentalist groups using public schools as their battleground' (Weil 2004). The interesting point here is the refashioning of a necessarily freedom-restricting law into one that protects individual liberties. Weil is aware of the price to be paid for this: 'I admit that the unfortunate consequence of the law passed by the French Parliament is that the right of Muslim girls who want to wear freely the scarf in public schools without pressuring anyone is denied' (ibid.). Weil thus rightly points to the one loser of the anti-headscarf law: the female Muslim pupil freely choosing to wear the headscarf. According to the sociological literature (especially Babés 1997), the autonomous headscarf, which debunks the notion that 'communitarian' pressures are behind the headscarf, had long become standard among young Muslim pupils. Indeed, the one publicly noted headscarf incident during the making of the 2004 law, that of Lila and Alma Levy, siblings of Jewish and non-practising Muslim parents, was one where the headscarf clearly stood for 'adolescent self-assertion or rebellion' (Laurence and Vaisse 2006: 166). Why not suppress baseball caps or baggy trousers, then? The suppression of the headscarf rested on an objective reading of it as oppressing women, which thus erased all alternative meanings. These alternative meanings may be spurious and idiosyncratic from the point of view of Islamic doctrine, but they fall within the ambit of religious liberty rights.

It is also interesting to note that a rather draconian and liberty-restricting measure was presented as one which respected the 'diversity' of society; it even figured as a demonstration of the 'open and generous' laicity that, in reality, was thrown out by this law. Thus the Stasi Report (2003: 16) characterized the need of the day to be one of 'forging unity *while respecting the diversity of society*' (emphasis added). And a socialist deputy in the Assemblée Nationale still claimed to be in favor of the 'open and generous laicity' (which, to repeat, was laid to rest in this law) after stating that, for 'republicans', laicity could 'not be reduced to tolerance' and that the veil had to be repressed for the sake of the 'unique singularity' of the school as a sacrosanct public space.[25] Similarly, President Jacques Chirac's ceremonial call for a law on laicity in front of a grand audience in the Elysée Palace, just two days after the publication of the Stasi Report, went to argue at great length that the proscription of 'ostensible' religious symbols in public schools was consonant with the respect for 'diversity' and with an 'open and generous' laicity, which 'guarantees the freedom of conscience'.[26] This attests to the hegemony of a liberal, rights-centered understanding of laicity, even though a rights-negating content was pushed through in a law that was more reminiscent of the republican 'combat' laicity of the past.

If one scrutinizes the parliamentary debate surrounding the law, one notices a striking absence of substantive disagreement. This is also visible in the voting outcome: after the first reading of the bill, 494 deputies of the National Assembly voted in favor, 36 voted against, and 31 abstained, the only party division in this being that communist deputies tended to oppose the law. After Prime Minister Raffarin set the tone of the debate with his opening remark that the purpose of the proposed law was nothing less than assuring 'the permanence of our values',[27] speaker after speaker, in numbing, ritualistic monotony, rallied to defend laicity in plainly nationalist terms: as 'French specificity' (MP Clément), as 'principle of "living together" in the republican way' (MP Asensi), as 'constitutive of our collective history' (MP Bur), as 'principal factor of the moral or spiritual unity of our nation [. . .] our social contract [. . .] heart of the republican pact' (MP Vaillant), as ' "sacred" value [. . .] of our republic' (MP Gerin), as 'cornerstone of republican values' (MP Brard), as 'essential part of our common national patrimony' (MP Paul), as 'founding principle of our republic' (MP Dionis du Séjour), and so on.[28]

The only significant disagreement arose with respect to the precise wording of the prohibition of religious symbols: should it cover all 'visible' or only 'ostentatious' symbols? The two commission reports came out with different recommendations in this respect. The parliamentary Debré Commission opted for 'visible'; the Stasi Commission preferred 'ostensible', thus anticipating the final outcome. Overall the socialists went for the more restrictive 'visible', because only this provided an objective standard which released local state agents from the difficulty of establishing the subjective intention behind the veil. However, as Marcel Long and Patrick Weil pointed out in an influential newspaper article – published a few days before the first reading of the bill and strategically placed in the leftist *Libération* – the problem of 'visible' was that it did not conform to the European Convention on Human Rights, whose Article 9 guarantees 'the liberty to manifest one's religion'.[29] In consequence, the preference finally shown for '*ostensible*' – which was a linguistic compromise between '*visible*', preferred by the socialists, and '*ostentatoire*', which represented the legal *status quo ante* – was conditioned by the fear of a European Human Rights Court intervention against France.

What was the precise difference between *ostensible*, *ostentatoire*, and *visible*? A Gaullist deputy who expressed the dominant view (which favored *ostensible* over its alternatives) explained that *ostensible* expressed 'the wish to be seen', and all the signs that were objectively exteriorized were covered by this description irrespective of the subjective intention of the person who carried the sign; *ostentatoire* (the legal status quo under the Bayrou *décret*) would entail 'a wish to provoke', which was too subjective and 'imprecise' to be workable; and, finally, *visible* was too 'restrictive of liberties', so that it too had to be discarded for fear of a court intervention.[30] These semantic disquisitions show that an astonishing degree of semiotic competence is asked of ordinary law-makers in the age of constitutional politics; more specifically, one sees that the socialists favored an even more restrictive law than the one which was eventually passed.

The 2004 Law on Laicity fundamentally reversed the legal regime which was in place until then. Before the law, under the aegis of a rights-centered, liberal laicity, tolerating the veil was the rule, prohibiting it was the exception. After the law, prohibiting the veil has become the rule and allowing it is the exception, under the aegis of a republican laicity which aims at national unity and cohesion at the inevitable cost of violating certain individual rights. The only major dissenter within the French political elite, the then Minister of Interior Sarkozy, argued that the law amounted to 'modifying the French concept of *laïcité*', because this had traditionally consisted in 'recognizing the right of religion' – so that 'it isn't the child that has to be laic but the school'.[31] This was true in the sense that the neutrality component of laicity had previously not applied to pupils but only to teachers; it was *not* true in the sense that the element of conformity to republican norms had been the 'other' side of laicity from the start.

What has been the impact of the French anti-headscarf law? Representative for many, Fadela Amara, the iconic leader of the feminist movement '*Ni putes ni soumises*', which attacked the repressive Islamism of the *banlieues*, fathomed that it could only fuel Islamic militancy: 'The reaction of the young is likely to be terrible [. . .] Instead of the veil one will impose *burkas* on certain women' (quoted in Gresh 2004: 262). Quite the opposite occurred. At the much feared *rentrée* (beginning of the school year) in September 2004, only 639 pupils showed up with a headscarf, and only 100 refused to take it off; one year later, there were only twelve counted headscarves nationwide on the first day of school (Laurence and Vaisse 2006: 171). Ironically, transnational Islam, the beast to beat in the 2004 headscarf law, helped to bring about a true *fraternité républicaine*[32] at the 2004 *rentrée*: the spectacular kidnapping of two French journalists by radical Islamists in Iraq, who demanded a repeal of the French headscarf ban, provoked an unprecedented closing of ranks behind the French state. 'There will be no blood on my headscarf', declared the leader of the Paris Mosque, quoting an unnamed Muslim girl (ibid. p. 171). At this critical moment, when the national allegiance of French Muslims was tested, they passed the test with flying colors, advancing from 'victims' to 'heroes' of the republic (*Le Monde*, quoted ibid., p. 171). Indeed, as Laurence and Vaisse rightly conclude (p. 172), the ultimate acceptance of the headscarf ban by French Muslims 'revealed the depth of integration and nationalization of Islam in France'.

3   The Teacher's Headscarf in Christian–Occidental Germany

Apart from France, Germany is the only country in Europe today that has legislated against the Islamic headscarf. The German justification for this has been similar to the French: the headscarf is outlawed primarily not as a religious but as a political symbol, that is, on account of its rejection of liberal–democratic precepts.[1] 'The headscarf [. . .] also stands for cultural segregation [*Abgrenzung*], and thus it is a political symbol [which puts at risk] social peace', argued Baden-Württemberg's Minister of Education Annette Schavan in the opening salvo of the German headscarf controversy.[2]

Underneath this common feature, however, there are two important differences. First, the social category targeted by German headscarf bans is that of teachers, not of pupils. Conversely, it was never questioned that the pupil's headscarf should be protected by religious liberty rights, according to Article 4 of the Basic Law. Teachers, however, as representatives of the state, were expected to exhibit 'distance' and 'neutrality' in matters of religious and ideological (*weltanschaulich*) expression, an attitude which was deemed to be violated by the donning of a headscarf (see Goerlich 1999).

Secondly, for the most part the German headscarf bans (of which there are several, because in German federalism education is under the control of regional governments) target Islam specifically, and explicit exemptions are made for Christian symbols. Banning the headscarf was never intended to implant French-style *laïcité*, which is misunderstood in Germany as a generalized hostility to all things religious. To the extent that the declared purpose of German headscarf bans is to defend the neutrality of the liberal state, they also seem to say, 'our neutrality is Christian' (Oestreich 2004: 51). Upholding, in March 2000, Baden-Württemberg's refusal to employ Mrs Ludin, the Administrative Court of Stuttgart stated bluntly: 'From the value decision of the constitution of the *Land* it follows that non-Christian teachers can express their religious affiliation only *under narrower conditions* than Christian teachers' (p. 52; emphasis added). Indeed, Article 16 of the regional constitution stipulates the 'Christian character' of the public school (*Volksschule*).

However, this was also the last time that a German court upheld the notion that the German state (at any level, regional or federal) was a Christian state that had the license to be partial, 'for' Christianity and 'against' Islam. This residue of ethnic nationalism, in which a particularistic 'us' is set of which 'they' cannot be a part, was rejected in all the subsequent higher court rules on the headscarf. In fact, one can read the German headscarf controversy as a battle over the meaning of 'the German state': was it a liberal state obliged to treat the adherents of all religious creeds equally, or was it an ethnic state in which the 'Christian–occidental' majority had certain privileges which the Islamic minority did not enjoy? The first position was taken by constitution-watching courts, the second by popularly accountable regional parliaments legislating against the headscarf.

Compared with France's two decades of openly conducted political debate surrounding Islam, there has been much less of it in Germany. Until the headscarf laws would politicize it, the accommodation of Islam had mostly been delegated to the silent workings of the judicial system. The key mechanism for this has been provided by the personal liberty and religious liberty clauses in Articles 2 and 4 of the Basic Law, which are universally granted to all individuals, irrespective of their citizenship. The minutiae of court-driven Muslim integration in Germany – from the mandate granting prayer breaks at the workplace, allowing Muezzin calls before dawn, or exempting the ritual killing of animals from animal protection laws, to particularly drastic applications of 'cultural defense' in penal law – still await their chronicler.[3]

Particularly relevant to our purposes is the expansive reach of religious liberty rights in public education. If French courts were extremely reticent to grant exemptions from religiously incensed parts of the school curriculum, German courts showed much less hesitation about this. In a landmark rule of 1993, the Federal Administrative Court (FAC) decided that a twelve-year old Turkish female pupil had the right to stay away from coeducational sport instruction on the grounds that, among other religiously forbidden things, she would face the risk of 'losing' her headscarf and of being exposed to the 'tightly cut or fitting sports dress of boys'.[4] In court, the girl's parents openly declared that they did not wish the 'emancipation' of their daughter according to 'western standards' (Albers 1994: 987). Certainly, the religious rights of pupils and of their parents had to be reconciled with the educational mandate of the state (in judicial terms, a 'practical concordance' between both had to be reached).[5] However, German courts almost always subordinated the state mandate to religious rights, without meeting much resistance from cowardly state authorities.

In a typical decision, which approvingly cites the 1993 FAC landmark rule, the Upper Administrative Court of North Rhine-Westphalia held that a Muslim girl in 10th grade had the right to stay away from the annual class retreat (*Klassenfahrt*), because the 'permanent fear' of violating her religious duties – for instance the duty not to eat pork, or the duty to pray five times a day – would be comparable to the 'sickness-indicating situation of a partially psychically handicapped who could travel only with another person accompanying her [*Begleitperson*]'.[6] Apart from its bizarre analogy, this decision raised eyebrows because it implicitly endorsed the so-called 'Camel-Fatwa' by a local cleric, according to whom Koranic law did not allow a female Muslim to travel more than eighty-one kilometers away from home – which is the distance a camel could presumably walk in 24 hours – without a blood-related male chaperone (*Mahram*).

Overall, if schools failed to 'exhaust all available organizational possibilities' to accommodate Islamic precepts,[7] as in a world of finite resources they often did, Muslim parents had a free hand to withdraw their children from inconvenient parts of the public school curriculum. This had obvious implications for the cohesion and morale in German classrooms.[8] No wonder that, in such a permissive setting, no one ever questioned the right of pupils to wear the headscarf in the classroom.

The multicultural jurisdiction of German courts occurred in the context of a public school which was notionally 'Christian'. As in most European countries, the origins of German public education are religious. Having stripped their confessional character only in the 1970s, most German public schools took on the form of 'Christian communal schools' (*christliche Gemeinschaftsschulen*), not bound by any particular creed, but nevertheless 'rooted in Christian cultural traditions' (Avenarius 2002: 83). Representative for most other German regions (*Länder*), the Constitution of Baden-Württemberg stipulates that public schools are 'Christian in character' (Article 16. 3), and that they are to educate children 'on the basis of Christian and occidental educational and cultural values' (Article 16. 2). However, to make this compatible with religious liberty rights, which require the state to be neutral towards religion, the German Constitutional Court (*Bundesverfassungsgericht*) decided already in the 1970s that the 'Christian' component of the newly created 'Christian community schools' could be exercised only in a cultural, not a religious sense.[9]

But how should one draw the line between culture and religion? In the famous Kruzifix decision of 1995, the Constitutional Court drew the line with the Christian cross, declaring the latter 'inherently religious' (*Glaubenssymbol schlechthin*). Accordingly, the Bavarian school order which prescribed the installation of a cross in each of the state's public classrooms was unconstitutional because it 'forced' pupils to 'learn "under the cross"',[10] in violation of pupils' (and their parents') religious liberty rights (which also include the negative right *not* to be exposed to religious symbolism). Overall, due to the religious rights jurisdiction of Germany's higher courts, there was a steady withdrawal of Christian elements from German public schools – until the challenge of Islam would bring the issue of religion back on the table.

The strong religious rights provisions of the German constitution also left their imprint on the organizational (versus individual) track of accommodating Islam,[11] greatly restricting the German state's possibilities to be less than even-handed with respect to Islam as organized religion also. To achieve public corporation status (*Körperschaft des öffentlichen Rechts*) is generally considered to be the last frontier of accommodating Islam in Germany, at least in a formal–institutional sense. When this status was first created with an eye on the Christian churches in the Weimar constitution, which had dumped the previous construct of an official (Protestant) state church, it was a compromise between the French-oriented left, which had pushed for a wholesale privatization of religion, and the Catholic right, which wanted to retain the public power and status of the churches (see Walter 2005: 37). Originally, to grant the public corporation status to certain religions while denying it to others was a matter of 'social utility' for the state (p. 35). In the words of a conservative constitutional lawyer, in granting public corporation status to a religion, the state acts 'not altruistically but in its own interest' and for the sake of 'self-preservation': the 'constitutional state' has to privilege the 'Christian heritage' on which it is based (Hillgruber 1999: 547).

Indeed the German state has for a long time denied public corporation status to organized religions which were not sufficiently 'loyal' to the state. However, in its decision on Jehova's Witnesses, the German Constitutional Court crossed out this last remnant of statist reasoning in religious recognition.[12] It argued that the state could only expect organized religion to be 'respectful of the law' (*rechtstreu*), which is less than 'loyalty' to the state. 'Loyalty', the court pointed out, entails an 'inner disposition, a morality [*Gesinnung*], and not just an external behavior'. But the latter was all that a neutral state could ask of a corporation of public law (or, for that matter, of any organized group or individual). Accordingly, it was irrelevant that Jehova's Witnesses denounced the secular state as an 'instrument of Satan' and that it instructed its adherents not to vote or stand for office in this state. The status of corporation of public law, according to Article 137 of the Basic Law, concluded the court, was not the expression of a special 'nearness to the state'; instead it was a mere 'means to further unfold religious liberty'.[13] With this rule, a critic acknowledged, 'the freedom of religion evolves into a comprehensive basic right [*Gesamtgrundrecht*], which next to its individual rights component includes also a corporatist component' (Hillgruber 2001: 1348). Conversely, all attempts to preserve cultural–historical particularism on the part of the state through a selective distribution of public corporation status were crossed out. There are no longer any principled reasons (if there ever was one) why an Islamic organization could not attain public corporation status and thus enjoy exactly the same privileges that the Christian churches and the Jewish community in Germany already enjoyed.

However, factual hurdles can be every bit as handicapping as the legal hurdles of the past. The official position of the federal government is to 'welcome' a 'central organization' among German Muslims, which is the key condition for achieving public corporation status. At the same time, the German government, in contrast to the French government, refuses to support this process, using the formalistic argument that the 'right of religious self-determination' is standing in its way.[14] In fact, when – on the eve of the second German Islam Conference (an initiative of the Federal Minister of the Interior which was designed to foster 'dialogue' with Germany's three million Muslims) – the three main religious Muslim organizations in Germany, to the surprise of many, overcame old rivalries and founded the Coordination Council of Muslims (CCM) in April 2007, the German government responded coolly that the CCM represented at best 15 percent of the German Muslims, and the religiously conservative and politically suspicious at that.[15] Blowing the same horn, a well-known feminist Muslim critic denounced the CCM as an 'assembly of Muslim tribal leaders', who did not represent the views of the majority of secular Muslims in Germany.[16] But did they have to, as a condition for achieving public corporation status?

Wouldn't it be like making the legitimacy of the Catholic Church depend on its representing also the views of pop star Madonna?[17] Still, the fear that public corporation status would only empower the conservative factions of Islam is well-grounded. Showering fundamentalist groups which are in the index of the *Verfassungsschutz* with state-collected tax moneys; allowing them to instruct the Koran as an ordinary school subject, autonomously and at public expense; and giving them a seat in the supervisory council of German public radio and television (*Rundfunkrat*) – may not be the most obvious ways of forging 'German Muslims' or 'enlightened Muslims in our enlightened country', which is the declared purpose of German state policy towards Muslims.[18] But, if religious Muslims happen to espouse liberally dubious views,[19] there is little that the liberal state can do against it, much as it has now to collect church taxes for a group that considers its own tax collector the 'instrument of Satan'.

But who are the Muslims in Germany? 75 percent out of the three million Muslims in Germany are Turks, which a leading German Islam expert characterized as a 'German stroke of luck' (*deutscher Glücksfall*).[20] Indeed, in contrast to much shriller Muslim activism in neighboring European countries, particularly in the Netherlands, 'we have peace in our cities', writes Werner Schiffauer in the aftermath of the slaughtering of Dutch film maker Theo Van Gogh by a Dutch Muslim.[21] Not before the mid-1990s did claims-making on the part of Turkish Muslims occur in terms of their being 'Muslim' rather than 'Turkish', a shift that predictably coincided with their increasing adoption of German citizenship. Still, many a second or third-generation 'Turk' continues to perceive himself or herself as 'Turk' or 'foreigner' (*Ausländer*), even if he or she holds German citizenship (as it is increasingly likely after the liberalization of the nationality law in 1999). As a study of veiled women in France and Germany observes, the German interviewees' self-description in terms of 'foreigner' occurred quite matter-of-factly, 'without [their] even attributing negative connotations to it' (Amir-Moazami 2004: 234). On the contrary, veiled Muslim women in Germany often stressed the 'tolerant' and 'liberal' character of German society, particularly if compared with laic Turkey, where the veil is prohibited at school and university (p. 235). As Amir-Moazimi dryly adds (p. 232), veiling can hardly be the 'political' act it is generally held to be by headscarf foes, given the external self-positioning of veiled women with regard to German society and state (even though, one should add, a generically 'anti-western' stance is not excluded, perhaps even facilitated by this). The minimum to say is that there is no legacy of colonialism to harden, embitter, or unduly politicize the stance of Muslims toward the German state.

In line with this, the Jewish–Arabic conflict in the Middle East, arguably the driving force behind the worldwide politicization of Islam, has found little resonance among Turkish Muslims in Germany. 'The actors of political Islam are not Turks. Jihad is not Turks' business. Palestine is not the problem of Turks', said a Turkish–German businessman (quoted in Yurdakul and Bodemann 2006: 51). A recent report by the International Crisis Group (2007) confirms that 'Islamic activism appears to be confined to the non-Turkish Muslim element' (p. 1). When the Turks in Germany turned towards addressing host-society concerns, particularly after the wave of xenophobic violence in the early 1990s, they used the 'German Jewish trope as a master narrative' (p. 52), comparing the arsonist attack in Mölln in 1992 (in which a Turkish woman and her two small children died) to the 'Holocaust' and sloganeering 'we don't want to be the Jews of tomorrow' (ibid). Even some of the new organizational labels such as *Türkische Gemeinde* or *Zentralrat der Muslime in Deutschland* are modeled on the Jewish example, as there already existed a *Jüdische Gemeinde* and a *Zentralrat der Juden in Deutschland*. These discursive and organizational borrowings from the German Jews are complemented by the Muslims' seeking the personal support of the Jewish leadership (which is notably not reciprocated by the latter: ibid., p. 60). In sum, the Turkish–Jewish rapprochement helps to prevent Islam from becoming the domestic security concern that it has undoubtedly become in France, Britain, or the Netherlands.[22]

Organized Islam in Germany originally duplicated the intra-Turkish political scene, with the laicist DITIB umbrella organization of mosques (the biggest in Germany) representing the official Turkish state Islam and Milli Görüs (Germany's second largest mosque organization) representing a fundamentalist Scharia-Islam, which had until recently been outlawed in Turkey. Directly opposed to both are secular organizations such as the *Türkische Gemeinde in Deutschland* or the *Türkischer Bund Berlin-Brandenburg* (TBB), which mobilize Turks on the basis of their national origins, with a primary focus on host society concerns. From the mid-1990s, even the religious organizations increasingly turned towards host society concerns. With respect to Milli Görüs, which now encourages its members to adopt German citizenship, to send girls to higher schools, and to practise Koran instruction in the German language, its leading chronicler speaks of a 'hidden assimilation' (*hintergründige Anpassung*), whereby originally strategic adjustments may grow over time into sincerely held convictions (Schiffauer 2003: 156).

This motley organizational picture makes for highly variegated positions in the German headscarf controversy. DITIB, torn between its official laicism and its religious nature, refused to take any position. The *Türkische Gemeinde* vehemently spoke out in favor of prohibiting all religious symbols in public schools. Only Milli Görüs (in terms of its national-level organization, the Islamrat) and the (Arab-based) *Zentralrat der Muslime in Deutschland* supported the headscarf (including its central protagonist, Fereshta Ludin), but both stood at best for an 'orthodox minority among German Muslims' (Oestreich 2004: 102).

The German headscarf controversy can be understood even less than the French as a massive movement of veiled women supported by vigilant Islamic organizations. Instead, the German controversy was a top-down product of judicial politics, which was galvanized by a single, protracted court case, that of Fereshta Ludin.

The remainder of this chapter first introduces the notions of 'open neutrality' and 'Christian–occidental', in terms of which Islam and its headscarf have been processed in Germany; secondly, it scrutinizes the Constitutional Court's seminal headscarf rule of September 2003, which triggered the anti-headscarf legislation of the *Länder*; and, thirdly, it examines this legislation's most pertinent feature: that of upholding a 'Christian–occidental' definition of the German state.

Open Neutrality and the Christian–Occidental State in Germany

If the French and British headscarf controversies were processed within opposite strands of liberalism, which stressed ethical perfectibility and toleration, respectively, the German case is situated both within *and* outside liberalism.

Squarely inside liberalism is the German variant of 'open' or 'comprehensive' neutrality (Böckenförde 2001: 725). In contrast to French *laïcité*, in which state and religion are strictly separated, German open neutrality asks the state to assure that individuals can express and live out their religious convictions not just in private but also in public; and religious associations, to the degree that they qualify as churches, are endowed with important public functions in education, in social service provision, and in health care. Because in this variant of neutrality the state welcomes and embraces religion, neutrality is reduced to a requirement that the state does not identify with any one religion, and that all religions in society are treated in an even-handed and impartial way. A Green Party opponent of outlawing the teacher's headscarf (who still identified with the German variant of open neutrality) described the ideal posture of the state in apposite terms: 'The state is not judge over the correct religion but umpire who has to make sure that all religions can prosper freely.'[23]

While possible in theory, the impartial embracing of religion is difficult to achieve in practice. This is where the 'Christian–occidental' trope kicks in, which pushes the German case outside the ambit of liberalism. To the degree that the German state is identified as 'Christian–occidental', Islam has no place in it. No such crypto-nationalist trope is discernible in France or Britain, neither of which has posited (at least not within their respective political mainstreams) a Christian 'us' of which an Islamic 'them' could not by definition be part. At one level, the 'Christian–occidental' trope is a substitute for the shattered idiom of ethnic nationhood.[24] But there is also a long tradition of the German state understanding itself not in terms of revolution but of evolution, as a secularized product of a specific (Christian) religious tradition. In particular, there has been a close relationship between nation-building and Protestantism. As a leading German historian writes about nineteenth-century Prussia, 'the Prussian reformers understood themselves, in explicit contrast to the French revolution, in religious terms; they wanted to ground state and society on a religious rebirth. And the emergent national movement is [. . .] just because of that religious, especially Protestant.'[25] In such a context, there must be an inherent inclination to treat 'impartiality' as an extraneous liberal norm which interferes with the vocation of the state to reproduce a particular tradition.

From this perspective, which is that of the conservative proponents of a selective exclusion of the Islamic headscarf, French-style laicity figured as *la bête noire* of a 'society without values': 'Laicism is the wrong way. A society without values is a worthless [*wertlose*] society. We are a society that has been marked by the Occident and by Christian values.'[26] What this deputy did not see is that laicity, of course, is a 'value' in France, a value defining the secular republic against the Catholic monarchy. Certainly, in contrast to the 'Christian–occidental' trope, laicity is a value that in principle everyone, irrespective of her religious or ethnic background, could subscribe to. In Germany, where there has been no identity-providing act of revolutionary founding, the 'values' of the state are not self-generated but they feed from external sources, most notably religion. In this sense, the close contact between state and religion secures for the state the moral resources it cannot itself provide. The underlying motif is expressed in Joseph von Eichendorff's famous notion, put forward at the Hambacher Fest of 1832, that 'no constitution [. . .] is self-perpetuating' (*Keine Verfassung [. . .] garantiert sich selbst*). This has been reiterated in E. W. Böckenförde's oft-quoted phrase that the 'secular [*freiheitliche*] state lives off conditions that it cannot itself guarantee' (1967). To a conservative lawyer and government advisor in the German anti-headscarf legislations, this suggests that the state remained dependent on close contact with *those* religions that have been the seedbed of the very process of secular constitution-making.[27]

One realizes now a fundamental difference between the ways in which the Islamic headscarf has functioned as a mirror of identity in Germany and France. In France, a substantive self-definition in terms of republican and laic could not just be effortlessly reconciled with the procedural universalism of neutrality; it even redefined the latter in terms of an identity. By contrast, the requirements of neutrality and of Christian–occidental self-definition in Germany part ways: in realizing one, you have to violate the other. By the same token, neutrality, if implemented fully, would work here against a crypto-national self-definition as 'Christian–occidental'.

With respect to the Islamic headscarf, German law-makers faced two opposite possibilities. The first was to extend the German tradition of religion-embracing neutrality. This would mean accepting veiled Muslim teachers in public school, much as veiled Catholic nuns were already accepted in the same capacity. While this option only seemed to prolong the status quo, it was still bound to corrode the traditional Christian–occidental self-definition of the state, because teachers with the Islamic headscarf would now become a common sight. As a legal observer aptly characterized the probable effect of tolerating veiled public school teachers, 'everyone who has eyes to see' would 'recognize the thinning of the ties that still hold this state together'.[28]

The second possibility was to move toward a stricter French-style neutrality. In this posture the state outlaws the headscarf but then would have to prohibit *all* religious symbolisms, the Christian ones included. On this second option, the corroding effect of neutrality on national self-definition was even more evident, as the state was now forced to abandon its self-description as Christian–occidental. Accordingly, whatever the state chose to do with respect to the headscarf, a certain distancing from self-definition of this sort was inevitable. This is because neutrality, on whatever reading, is incompatible with not treating all religions equally. Strikingly, German anti-headscarf laws denied the existence of the dilemma, notionally being in defense of the neutrality of the state but in reality violating it through selectively excluding Islamic (but not Christian) symbols.

For Religious Liberty and Neutrality: The Constitutional Court's Headscarf Decision

The necessity to legislate on the headscarf arose with the Constitutional Court's landmark decision, in September 2003, on the case of Fereshta Ludin, who had been denied the civil servant job of school teacher in the *Land* of Baden-Württemberg because she refused to take off her headscarf in the classroom. Born in Afghanistan in 1972 and a naturalized German citizen since 1995, Mrs Ludin predictably defended herself by appealing to the German tradition of open neutrality, which would entitle her to wear the Islamic veil for 'personal' and 'religious' reasons. Her denial of a political dimension to her wearing a headscarf was a bit hypocritical, because she moved in the Islamist environment of Milli Görüs and of the *Zentralrat der Muslime in Deutschland* (ZMD), which financed her lawsuit, and in such circles she once described the headscarf as 'protection from western decadence' (Oestreich 2004: 116).

It was nevertheless legitimate on Mrs Ludin's part to try mobilizing the German way of handling religion. If school prayer was allowed, she argued, and teachers undoubtedly engaged in it as a religious practice, the headscarf had to be allowed too. More generally, in the tradition of 'comprehensive, open, and respecting neutrality', the school should not be an extra-societal 'refuge' but a mirror of society's pluralism, having the mandate to 'prepare young people for what they will encounter in society'. Accordingly, in reprimanding her for a violation of the neutrality mandate of the state, the state had actually shifted towards a 'strict' understanding of neutrality, which was rather reminiscent of a 'laicist state' and in deviation from the German tradition.[29]

The Federal Administrative Court (FAC), in its 4 July 2002 decision, which sanctioned Mrs Ludin's loss of her job, had indeed taken a French neutrality line: 'In a plural society [the state] must pay respect to very diverse parental opinions, and it has to refrain from any religious indoctrination by teachers. Therefore the neutrality mandate becomes more important with the increase of cultural and religious diversity, and this mandate is not – as the plaintiff holds – to be loosened up in reference to the fact that the cultural, ethnic, and religious diversity in Germany is now shaping life in the school also.'[30]

The reasoning of the Federal Administrative Court goes to the heart of the question of how the liberal state should deal with religious and cultural difference: should the state reflect and acknowledge this difference or should it keep it at bay, for the sake of a more equitable balancing of the diverse interests and claims which are now impinging on it? Overall, in repressing the headscarf, the French and the German state have both opted for the second answer, though with differing nuances. In France, this repression was conceived of as a matter of *vivre ensemble* as against *vivre côté à côté* (Debré Rapport 2003: tome 1, partie 1ère, p. 42), that is, as a matter of assuring national unity in a centrifugal society.

In Germany, a lawyerly idiom of balancing between different rights titles was predominant. In constitutional law terms, a 'practical concordance' (*praktische Konkordanz*) had to be achieved between conflicting rights and interests: first, the right of the teacher to the 'freedom of belief' and to 'equal access to public office', guaranteed by Articles 4 and 33 of the Basic Law; secondly, the right of school children to 'negative' religious freedom, that is, the right not to be indoctrinated by teachers; thirdly, the 'natural right' of parents to educate their children, guaranteed by Article 6 of the Basic Law; and, fourthly, the public education and neutrality mandate of the state. The regional government of Baden-Württemberg, as well as all court instances up to the FAC, had argued that the teacher's rights had to take second place, giving way to the 'more vulnerable' position of students and parents. These were inescapably exposed to the powers of the state, while the latter was seen as acting through its teachers: 'The increased need for protection on the part of children in primary and secondary school, who are mostly not yet old enough to chose religion [*religionsmündig*], has priority over the right of the teacher to express her religion in public.'[31] Conversely, the teacher's individual rights were curtailed by her role as agent of the state, which obliged her to carry out the state's mandate of 'religious and ideological neutrality'.[32]

With the stroke of a pen, the Constitutional Court's September 2003 decision nullified all previous court rules and government decisions on the Ludin case, arguing that the teacher's unconditionally granted constitutional rights could not be restricted without a statutory basis, which did not exist in this case. Arguably one of the most criticized, even ridiculed, decisions ever made by the German Constitutional Court, this was at heart a self-denying, anti-'juristocracy' rule, which held that not the courts but the political branches of the state, most importantly the democratic legislature, should decide about a socially and politically contested issue, namely how to deal with religious and cultural difference. The law-maker was essentially free to treat the religious diversity in school as 'means for the learning of [*Einübung von*] mutual tolerance', and thus to tolerate the headscarf even of teachers; *or* to shift towards a 'stricter and more distancing' understanding of state neutrality.[33] However, if the French-style 'distancing' option was taken, as it apparently was in Baden-Württemberg's refusal to employ Mrs Ludin, a statutory law was necessary. Such a statutory basis, in terms of a law on neutrality or of a revised education law, which in the German federal state falls under the jurisdiction of regional governments, was 'also' required 'because [. . .] the members of different religious communities had to be treated equally in this respect'.[34] This was a clear hint that a law on neutrality or a revised education law could not selectively target the headscarf but would have to exclude from the school, equally, *all* religious symbols. This is the one tenet of the Constitutional Court's headscarf decision which all the subsequent anti-headscarf laws of the *Länder* would blatantly disregard (with the single exception of that of Berlin).

At the same time, the Constitutional Court left no doubt that, within the traditional understanding of an 'open' neutrality, veiled teachers had to be tolerated. In fact, much of the court's written decision is spent on dispelling public fears and prejudices about the headscarf. First, the court argued that, 'considering the multiplicity of motivations [for wearing a headscarf], the headscarf must not be reduced to a sign of the oppression of women', and that in the case of genuine religious motivation the act of veiling was protected by Article 4 of the Basic Law.[35] Interestingly, subsequent anti-headscarf laws drew the exact opposite conclusion from the basic datum of the 'multiplicity of motivations': on account of this multiplicity, the headscarf *could* be taken as a political statement on the inequality of women, which violated the principles of the Basic Law and justified banning the headscarf. This is how Annette Schavan, Minister of Education in Baden-Württemberg, justified her anti-headscarf bill before the *Landtag*: 'The veil as a political symbol is also part of a history of oppressing women [. . .] So it is not reconcilable with a constitutional value that is anchored in our Basic Law.'[36]

Secondly, the court made a subtle distinction between the 'state' and the 'teacher' acting in its name: 'The state, which accepts [*hinnimmt*] the religious statement implicit in the wearing of the headscarf by a teacher, does not thereby identify with this statement.'[37] This reveals a fundamental question raised by the veiling debate: Who is the state? For the opponents of the veil, the teacher *is* the state, and thus he or she should appear to be neutral. Headscarf opponents drew their ammunition, in unison, from the Constitutional Court's 1995 Kruzifix rule, equating the state-ordered crucifix on the school wall with the teacher's headscarf. However, a legal critic commented that 'the headscarf of a teacher is an expression of her individual beliefs, which cannot be attributed to the state' (Sackofsky 2003: 3299). Moreover, with respect to the state, a minimal distinction can be made between the immediate exercise of sovereignty, as in the cases of judges and police officers, and the regulation of social life, as in the case of educators and health care or social workers, which could in principle be provided also in a non-state form, through market or civil society. As E.W.Böckenförde (1973) pointed out in an early treatise on the constitutional validity of school prayer, different forms of neutrality should apply to each state function: 'distancing' or 'strict' neutrality in the case of the sovereignty function, and 'open' or 'comprehensive' neutrality in the case of social regulation. Something similar to this proposal is hinted at in the court's differentiation between 'state' and 'teacher'.

Thirdly, the court pointed out that 'not enough knowledge' (*ungesicherte Erkenntnislage*) existed with respect to the psychological effect of the headscarf on uniformed school children. In light of this, the restriction of a fundamental right of the plaintiff was not warranted.[38] In fact one psychologist audited by the court opined that for the children the headscarf was at most 'funny clothing', akin to what 'grandmother wears in *Kasperletheater*', and it certainly did not incite conscious emulation.[39]

Within the Constitutional Court itself, the Ludin decision was highly contested and only five out of eight justices supported it. In an unusual move in German court practice, the three disagreeing justices had their minority opinion attached to the decision. According to the minority justices, the fundamental flaw of the court majority was to 'ignore the functional limitation of individual rights protection for civil servants'.[40] Basic constitutional rights, which were invoked by the court majority in favor of the plaintiff, are by nature negative rights of defense, which only apply when the state uninvitedly intrudes in the life of individuals. By contrast, in the case at hand 'not public power is invading society, but a carrier of basic rights is seeking nearness to the state',[41] so that the entire construct of constitutional rights protection does not apply. On the contrary, civil servants have essentially waived the constitutional rights that are incompatible with their office, and they are obliged to 'temperance and professional neutrality'.[42] Furthermore, no special law was required to assure the civil servant's neutrality, as the latter followed from the constitutionally prescribed requirements of public service itself: '[U]ncompromisingly insisting on wearing a headscarf while teaching in a public school, as the plaintiff has done, is not compatible with the imperative of moderation and neutrality required of a civil servant.'[43]

Indeed, since Max Weber's classic sociology of the state, in which a 'charismatic' political leadership is juxtaposed to an 'impersonal' bureaucracy, the latter was to act *sina ira et studio* and impartially administer the office (Weber 1977: 27f). From this perspective, the neutrality of the teacher as public servant of the state is not so much a reflection of the neutrality of the liberal state: the state leadership *had* to be partial and stance-taking, as this is the very meaning of 'politics'. Rather, neutrality is a reflection of the professional ethos of the subaltern civil servant. In the decision of the majority justices, this ethos is evidently subordinated to the constitutional rights attributed to the office holder. Accordingly, constitutional lawyer Josef Isensee characterized the majority decision as 'rights activism and office amnesia': 'Office is service, not realization of the self. This *Askese* is the price for partaking in state power.'[44]

Overall, the Constitutional Court's headscarf decision amounted to a strong protection of religious liberties and a reinforcement of liberal neutrality, in the sense of treating Islam like any other religion. And in 'Christian-occidental' Germany this did not come as easily as in 'laicist' France.

Resurrection of the 'Christian–Occidental' State in the Political Sphere

The Constitutional Court's decision on 'Ludin' had a staggering political impact: all existing regulations on religious symbols in public schools were immediately nullified, without a transitional period, and state governments intent on prohibiting the headscarf for teachers were required to pass legislation in that respect instantly. In one legal critic's view, the 'court has needlessly raised a difficult political dispute' (Campenhausen 2004: 666), and this in a moment of high tension surrounding the role of Islam in the western world.

The Catholic Church and political figures across party-lines, such as former Bavarian Minister of Education Hans Maier

(CSU) and then Federal President Johannes Rau (SPD), publicly spoke out against anti-headscarf legislation, fearing that
all religions would now be forced to retreat into the private
sphere. In a widely noted speech honoring the 275th birth-
day of the great liberal Enlightenment figure and religious
toleration icon G. E. Lessing, President Rau argued that a
selective targeting of the Islamic headscarf for exclusion was
not reconcilable with the equal religious liberties guaranteed
by the Basic Law. Accordingly, 'a headscarf ban would be the
first step on the road toward a laicist state, which removes
religious signs and symbols from public life. This is not my
idea of a country which has been shaped by Christianity for
many centuries.'[45] Rau's equation of crucifix and headscarf
was immediately rebutted by Cardinal Ratzinger: 'I would not
prohibit a Muslim woman from wearing the headscarf, but
even less are we prepared to accept prohibition of the cross,
which is the public symbol of a culture of reconcilia-
tion' (quoted in Informationszentrum Asyl und Migration
2004: 24).

Indeed, with the exception of Berlin, the anti-headscarf legislation passed in seven other *Länder* (Baden-Württemberg,
Bavaria, Hesse, Lower Saxony, Saarland, and more recently
Bremen and North Rhine-Westphalia) more or less explicitly
exempted Christian and Jewish religious symbols from its
reach.[46] It is not far-fetched to explain this variation in party-
political terms. The Berlin Law on the Ideological Neutrality
of the State, which is the only law prohibiting *all* religious
symbols, Christian and Jewish ones included, was passed by
a leftist coalition government of social democrats (SPD) and
former communists (PDS). All other laws, which contain
exemptions for Christian and Jewish symbols, were passed by
the conservative, Christian–Democratic Party (CDU/CSU) or
'great coalition' governments. The left/right schism on this
matter, with the right always favoring the selective exclusion
of Islam and the left refusing to single out Islam for exclusion,
is affirmed by the case of North Rhine-Westphalia. As long as
it was ruled by the SPD, North Rhine-Westphalia had remained
the only state which explicitly rejected anti-headscarf legislation despite the presence of at least fifteen teachers wearing

headscarves in classrooms of this *Land*. This was to set a counterpoint of 'toleration' to the restrictive attitude prevailing in the conservatively ruled *Länder* (Campenhausen 2004: 667, n. 8). Conversely, one of the first things an incoming CDU government would do in North Rhine-Westphalia in 2006 was to pass a selectively exclusive headscarf law.

Most anti-headscarf laws, with their selective targeting of the Islamic headscarf, follow the model of Catholic–conservative Baden-Württemberg, the state of origin of the German headscarf debate. It is thus apposite to look at this case more closely. Baden-Württemberg's anti-headscarf legislation consists in including three new sentences into Paragraph 38 of the state's education law. These new sentences, as formulated in the original bill, are as follows:[47]

Box 3.1

SENTENCE 1 'Teachers are not allowed [. . .] to give external statements [*äussere Bekundungen*] of a political, religious [or] ideological nature which could endanger or disturb the neutrality of the *Land* towards pupils or parents or [. . .] the political, religious or ideological peace of the school.'

SENTENCE 2 'Especially impermissible is an external behavior which could create the impression, in pupils or parents, that a teacher opposes the equality [principle] according to Article 3 of the Basic Law, basic liberty rights, or the liberal–democratic order.'

SENTENCE 3 'The representation of Christian and occidental values or traditions corresponds to the educational mandate of the [regional] constitution and does not contradict the behavior required [*Verhaltensgebot*] according to Sentence 1.'

Sentence 1 stresses the abstract possibility of 'endangering' or 'disturbing' neutrality; no special examination is required as to whether the 'external statements' *really* have this effect.

Accordingly, this is a law that excludes point blank, without consideration of any specific case. Sentence 2 has been labeled by the legal advisor of the regional government as 'the headscarf sentence':[48] it shall allow singling out the headscarf over all other religious symbols for its *political* dimension of opposing certain liberal–democratic values, most notably equality between the sexes. Sentence 2 is also a concession to the German tradition of religion-embracing neutrality, in that religious symbols are not prohibited per se, but only if they have detrimental political implications. Furthermore, Sentence 2 disregards the subjective intention behind the headscarf and stresses its objective meaning for the audience. As the government's legal advisor put it, 'symbols have an intrinsic meaning (*Eigenwert*), as every corporate logo has. It does not matter what the user of the symbol intends.'[49] Finally, the single most contested part of the entire legislation, Sentence 3, explicitly exempts Christian and Jewish symbols from the reach of the law. It achieves this by means of a subtle distinction between the 'representation' of religion as a distinct national tradition, which the state was constitutionally obliged to uphold, and the identification with, and propagation of, a religion which the state – qua neutral state – was never allowed to engage in. In a nutshell, if transformed from religion into culture, the Christian religion could be privileged without violating the neutrality mandate. Sentence 3 encapsulates the main purpose of the law, which a member of the Liberal Democratic Party (FDP) flatly characterized thus: 'We prohibit the headscarf and simultaneously affirm symbols that have shaped our occident'.[50]

The selective prohibition of the headscarf, which distinguishes the German anti-headscarf laws from the French law on laicity, is evidently achieved by taking two separate angles: first, by prohibiting, not religious symbols as such, but only those which are said to carry objective political meaning – a class which, in effect, contains only the headscarf; and, secondly, by positing an explicit 'privilegium Christianum'. Each of these angles has subsequently been questioned for its constitutionality. With respect to the first, the minister of education of Baden-Württemberg declared: 'If the headscarf were an exclusively religious symbol, there would be no debate at all.'[51]

Accordingly, this law did not imply a change toward a 'stricter', 'distancing' neutrality, as it was laid out in *one* scenario of the Constitutional Court; instead, this law was notionally in continuation of the German tradition of 'open' and 'comprehensive' neutrality. As a CDU deputy clarified, 'it is *not* the motivation of this law to repress all religious symbolisms [*religiöse Bezüge*], in light of the increasing cultural, religious, and ideological diversity in our country'.[52]

Zeroing in on the political dimension of a religious symbol allowed invidious distinctions between the Christian cross and the Islamic headscarf: 'In contrast to the headscarf, the cross belongs to the culture of the occident, to our tradition, and it is cherished here as a religious testimony to altruism, tolerance, and the respect for human dignity.'[53] However, the singling out of the political dimension of religion could be achieved only over a certain contradiction: the 'polyvalence' (*Mehrdeutigkeit*) of the veil was admitted, or even presupposed, while the possibility of a religious meaning was subsequently removed (or at least rendered irrelevant) by legislative fiat. Strictly speaking, the 'polyvalence' of the veil would recommend a case-by-case evaluation, as was incidentally suggested by three out of the four constitutional lawyers audited by the *Landtag* of Baden-Württemberg.[54] This is exactly the road *not* taken in this (and all other German headscarf) law(s). As the constitutional lawyer Jestaedt testified before the *Landtag*, 'it is unconstitutional to ignore the interpretation of the teacher', because 'the teacher has constitutional rights'. In the fact that the teacher's own interpretation of the veil is ignored, she is 'degraded to an object of interpretation by others'.[55] This completely nullified the claims of one of the four parties between whom, according to the German legal–constitutional framing of the headscarf conflict, a 'practical concordance' had to be reached: the teachers. The only legal supporter of this nullification (who, incidentally, was advisor to the regional government) retorted to this objection: 'Balancing can also mean that in one area one basic right must step back completely.'[56] The choice of the view one took on this matter obviously depended on one's notion of what a 'teacher' is: an individual rights holder, like every citizen or person in the state, or a civil servant, whose individual rights are restricted for the sake of office-holding. Moreover, this debate closely resembled one known from literary theory: does the meaning of a symbol lie in the author's intention, in the audience's reception, or somewhere in between (as noted by Altinordu 2004: 13)?

The second, and even more contested, way to target the headscarf selectively consisted in the positing of a 'privilegium Christianum'. The license for this was derived from a decision of the Constitutional Court in 1975, which declared to be in accordance with the Basic Law the newly created public 'Christian community schools' (*christliche Gemeinschaftsschulen*) in the region of Baden, in which children were 'educated on the basis of Christian and occidental educational and cultural values'.[57] The plaintiffs, who had objected to a Christian education, had argued that this school form violated their religious liberties and the neutrality of the state. The court rejected this claim by making a distinction between the 'recognition [of Christianity] as a formative cultural and educational factor', which the state was not just permitted but constitutionally obliged to make, and the inculcation of 'credal truth', which the state, on account of its neutrality, was never allowed to undertake. In other words: the state could identify with the secularized aspects of Christianity, for instance with 'the idea of tolerating dissenters', but not with Christianity as a religious creed.[58]

The legal advisor of Baden-Württemberg denied that the use of this distinction in Sentence 3 of the revised Paragraph 38 of the Law on Education constituted a 'privilegium Christianum'; instead, it expressed a mere 'historical privilege' (F. Kirchhof, in Ausschuss für Jugend, Schule, und Sport 2004: 80). Christian symbols were permitted to the degree that they were not the 'expression of an identification with religion', but the 'expression of a national identity', thus having a mere 'historical value' (Kirchhof, ibid., p. 13). To illustrate this, he referred to the city emblem of Munich, which showed a monk in a brown cloak (*Kutte*): '[N]obody would say that the city of Munich is in any way favoring a religion here; instead, she is only performing her tradition' (ibid.). From this it followed that Catholic nuns teaching in public school in their uniform should continue to be allowed to do so, despite the revised education law: 'The nun's dress is, of course, admissible, because it corresponds to a historical formation [*historische Gestaltung*]' (p. 83).

The logic of this secularized 'privilegium Christianum' was paraphrased in popular language by constitutional lawyer Mahrenholz: '[T]he essence of the bill is that the VfB Stuttgart [the local first-division soccer team] is the traditional club here, and one is allowed to wear its dress in school; the dress of other teams is not allowed' (Ausschuss für Jugend, Schule, und Sport: 33). If this went with a smile, the more serious problem was that a secular interpretation of the Catholic nun's *Habit* violated the credal meaning which it surely had to have for her. As the audited constitutional lawyer Böckenförde ridiculed the proposed secular interpretation of the nun's dress, 'the nuns of Baden-Baden-Lichtental would certainly complain if told that they are a Christian folk dress club (*Trachtenverein*)' (p. 67). In the curious view of the regional government, and following a declaration of Catholic bishops, the nun's dress was admissible not just 'as culture', but also as 'legally protected work dress'.[59] Or, as Minister of Education Schavan varied the theme, the nun's dress was 'an expression of belonging to an estate [*Stand*], not an expression of personal belief'.[60]

Considerable legal acrobatics were required to achieve the desired result: to prohibit the Islamic but to allow the Catholic headscarf. However, one has to appreciate the dilemma that the headscarf issue posed to the German state. This was a state which had never defined itself in universalistic terms, as a French-style republic committed to human rights and ethnicity-blind citizenship. Instead, the particular national tradition forwarded by the German state at this point in time consisted of a commitment to 'Christian–occidental values'. And these values had to leave out Islam as a non-Christian, non-occidental cultural education. Such an exclusion was bound to invite the charge of a violation of constitutional equality and liberty rights. The need for reconciling both: observing constitutional equality and liberty rights *and* maintaining a distinct national tradition and identity, is eloquently expressed by Baden-Württemberg's minister of education in her final plea for a selective ban of the Islamic headscarf:

> In a religiously plural society [we have to] achieve both: first, assure that religious liberty is no monopoly of Christians; secondly, not pretend that every commitment to our own traditions and cultures – and these are nowhere in the world thinkable without religious roots – is *ipso facto* problematic in a religiously pluralizing society. These are the two sides of the one medal of a society which knows about its heart and fundament and which at the same time practises the world openness that has been achieved not least through the secularization of Christian values.[61]

And, with an eye on the current 'dialogue with Islam', which is known to despise western consumer culture, it would be detrimental if 'we [. . .] defined our identity through well-being, consumption, and materialism alone'.[62]

As real as the dilemma was, the violation of constitutional liberty and equality rights inherent in the solution chosen in most German anti-headscarf laws did not thereby disappear. As a Green deputy in the *Landtag* of Baden-Württemberg pointed out, 'it is completely contradictory to prohibit a teacher from expressing her political, religious, or ideological beliefs in reference to the neutrality of the state [. . .] and on the other hand to violate this neutrality through privileging Christianity as the traditional religion of the country'.[63] Indeed, on this peculiar understanding of 'neutrality', only 'the strangers' had to be neutral, while 'we' had the license to be partial.[64] In a revealing exchange, a Green deputy accused the anti-headscarf law's proponents of 'privileging the traditional [*angestammte*] religion through recourse to occidental educational and cultural values' – to which a CDU deputy loudly interjected 'Absolutely!'[65] This was the core of the matter, once the forced legal jargon was off.

Three of the four constitutional lawyers audited by the *Landtag* of Baden-Württemberg insisted that the 'privilegium Christianum' was not reconcilable with the federal constitution. Former constitutional justice Mahrenholz phrased it in the words of Faust's Mephisto: 'In the first choice you are free, in the second you are servant [*Knecht*]' (Ausschuss für Jugend, Schule, und Sport 2004: 39). That is, if the government accepted the nun's dress, it had to accept the Islamic headscarf; if, on the opposite, the headscarf was rejected, a 'privilegium Christianum' was not permissible either, and the nun's dress had to be rejected too. Constitutional lawyer Jestaedt pointed out the impossibility of allowing Christian religious symbols through the secular route, because such symbols, when worn by a person, had to be 'religiously intended', so that the critical Sentence 3 of the revised Paragraph 38 of Baden-Württemberg's Law on Education, which stipulated the 'credal'–'secular' distinction, was simply incapable of achieving the desired result (ibid., p. 56). And the most prominent legal critic of the German anti-headscarf laws, Böckenförde, foresaw that these laws, against their expressed intention, were 'pacemakers on the road toward laïcité in Germany', because their constitutionality hinged upon 'extending the prohibition to all religious expressions equally'.[66]

One sees that state neutrality in Germany, should it fully have its way, is forcing the state to distance itself from its own national tradition, to the extent that the latter is defined as 'Christian–occidental'. And the lever on this is the jurisdiction of constitutional courts, whose mandate is to guard the constitution's liberty and equality rights.

An Evolving Conflict

All eyes are now directed at how the courts will respond to the resurrection of the 'Christian–occidental' state in the anti-headscarf laws. Such a response will be a measure of the possibilities of the contemporary state to engage in particularistic nation-building. Even advocates of nation-building concede that the 'state of the Basic Law' may 'privilege Christian religion and occidental culture, which constitute its fundament, *only in very restricted ways*' (Hillgruber 1999: 546; emphasis added). In particular, the individual and religious liberty and equality clause in Basic Law Articles 2 to 4 'exclude the use of state power for the production of religious–cultural homogeneity' (p. 547). In a nutshell, if the constitution prevails, the German state cannot be a 'Christian–occidental' state.

Still, a first examination of Baden-Württemberg's anti-headscarf law by the Federal Administrative Court (FAC), in June 2004, is ambiguous in this respect. On the one hand it confirms, in the final instance, Baden-Württemberg's rejection of Mrs Ludin as a public school teacher. The FAC rule also confirms the constitutionality of the anti-headscarf law passed a few months earlier. Even the contested Sentence 3 of the revised Paragraph 38 of the state's Law on Education passes constitutional muster, because 'the representation of Christian and occidental educational and cultural values from a neutral perspective is different from the expression of an individual belief'.[67] But the court also stipulates: 'Exceptions for special forms of religiously motivated dress in certain regions [. . .] cannot be accepted [. . .] Material constitutional law would stand against this.'[68] While the court remained silent about the precise meaning of this phrase, the phrase itself has been interpreted by some as a plea for the strictly equal treatment of all religions, a plea thus invalidating the 'privilegium Christianum' as intended by the anti-headscarf law.[69] However, when asked by the Greens in parliament whether the final legal word on the Ludin case would have to be interpreted in this way, the regional government said 'no' and reiterated its known line: 'Nuns carry their *Habit* as an expression of belonging to an order. The dress represents a Christian tradition.'[70] The nagging question of how one can wear a nun's dress without expressing a belief remains. A sarcastic critic opined that to deny the religious virtuosi their belief and to degrade them to being 'mere custodians of our constitutional principles' marked the victory of a 'militant atheism, in alliance with the churches'.[71] This was the irony that had marked the German religious culture wars since the Constitutional Court's famous Kruzifix rule: the crypto-nationalist advocates of a state-level 'privilegium Christianum', like the wolf in the fairy-tale, had to eat chalk, and water down 'religion' as 'culture', while their liberal critics would thunder that reducing the crucifix to a mere 'expression of occidental tradition' amounted to a 'profanization' of the cross that 'contradicted the self-understanding of Christianity'.[72]

Three further court rules point in contradictory directions. In July 2006, the Administrative Court of Stuttgart confirmed a liberal reading of the 2004 FAC rule by allowing a Muslim teacher to wear a headscarf in class, despite and over

Baden-Württemberg's headscarf law of 2004. In its decision, the court referred to the fact that Catholic nuns were still allowed to wear their religious dress in class, so that a selective exclusion of the Islamic headscarf violated the equality principle of the Basic Law. (For an interesting critique of the rule's justification which still agrees with its substantive conclusion, see Bader 2006.)

By contrast, two reviews of the anti-headscarf laws in Bavaria and Hesse by their respective Constitutional Courts in 2007 reasserted the Christian privilege posited in both laws. In its examination of the Law to Secure State Neutrality in Hesse – which is the harshest of all German headscarf laws because it targets not only teachers but all civil servants – the Staatsgerichtshof simply denied that there was a 'privilegium Christianum' in this law. On the one hand, the court stipulated that Christian symbols, if exaggerated ('Key words: Christian fundamentalism, large conspicuous crosses worn as jewelry'), *could* be prohibited;[73] on the other hand, those symbols that merely expressed the 'Christian and humanist occidental tradition of the *Land*' were 'objectively unsuited' to impair 'trust in the neutrality' of the office holder.[74] Three justices disagreed, arguing that the law included an 'unconstitutional privileging of Christian dresses'.[75] In fact, the court's narrow six-to-five majority mirrored exactly the political constellation in Hesse: the five minority justices all belonged to the Social–Democratic Party, which formed the parliamentary opposition at the time, while the majority justices simply toed the line of the conservative government, which had appointed them in the first place and had passed the headscarf law.[76]

The German headscarf conflict is still evolving, until the case arrives that will force the Federal Constitutional Court either to confirm or to revoke its earlier insistence on treating all religions equally.

4 The Extreme Headscarf in Multicultural Britain

For a long time, Britain kept away from the headscarf controversies raging on the European continent. As this situation has recently changed, it is apposite to ask what made Britain so different once, and why controversy could not be avoided in the end. In a nutshell, the 'multicultural' accommodation of the Islamic headscarf had already happened when an extreme version of it, covering face and body, put it to the test. Britain had its first headscarf incidence back in 1989, the very year of the Foulard Affair in France, when the headmaster of Altrincham Girls' Grammar School, near Manchester, excluded two Muslim siblings who had refused to take off their headscarves in class. It was resolved in a quintessentially British way: the headscarf was allowed, provided that it came in dark blue – the colors of the school uniform. If one compares this first outcome with the far more combative scene in France, who would disagree that a 'speedy, sensible and pragmatic compromise was thus reached, without the issue having to be tested in the Courts' (Poulter 1997: 68)? Courts, however, did become centrally involved once the extreme headscarf, *jilbab* and *niqab* – which were claimed by pupils and teachers alike – questioned the multicultural arrangements that had been put in place precisely in response to the headscarf.

The first part of this chapter maps out the multicultural context of accommodating Islam in Britain. The second and third parts discuss the challenge of the extreme headscarf in the legal and political spheres, respectively.

British Multiculturalism Meets Islam

To understand how the Islamic headscarf could become a mirror of identity in Britain too, one must first explicate the distinct nature of British 'multiculturalism', which has provided the discursive and institutional context for the accommodation of Islam. While always cited as a show-case of multiculturalism in Europe, Britain has never espoused an official multiculturalist policy of the kind one can find in Canada or Australia – inscribed in statutory or even constitutional law, becoming part of the national self-definition, and immune to the whims of political partisanship. Instead, following a typically British pattern of evolution rather than revolution, British multiculturalism is a natural prolongation of British liberalism.

Consider that, in contrast to Canada or Australia, Britain never had a dramatic turning-point, setting a clear 'before' and 'after' the turn to multiculturalism. Roy Jenkins' famous abdication of 'assimilation' as a 'flattening process', in 1966, which is commonly taken to be the beginning of British multiculturalism *avant la phrase* (also by Joppke 1999: 225), marked no turning-point at all, because there had been no assimilation policy before that. Rather, this was the moment of British liberalism meeting the fact of racial pluralism at home. And the anti-discrimination or 'race relations' policy that followed was quintessentially liberal, taking the individual, not the group, as a unit of integration and seeking to render irrelevant rather than to perpetuate ascriptive group membership. In this sense, race relations policy – the alleged center-piece of British multiculturalism – was not multicultural at all. In fact, no government before New Labour had ever taken up multicultural rhetoric. The preceding conservative government, under Thatcher, had even conducted a war against the socialism of the Greater London Authority, whose militant 'anti-racism' was multicultural not in word but in spirit. Indeed, British multiculturalism became a hard fact only at sub-national level, where local authority structures in areas of dense minority settlement, like London or the British Midlands, proved highly permeable to minority group claims.

But what is British liberalism? It is a variant of liberalism that prioritizes private choice and non-interference over public 'character-building' (see Levinson 1997). Inherent in liberalism is a tension between toleration and ethical perfection (see Gray 2000), with Britain and France institutionalizing variants of – respectively – toleration and perfection. If confronted with the fact of pluralism, each variant of liberalism is potentially self-destructive: toleration liberalism is eroded by the paradox of tolerating the intolerant, while ethical liberalism turns illiberal by evicting the merely private from a homogenized public space.

Evolving out of toleration liberalism, British multiculturalism lacks a public dimension. It is private choice applied to the fact of pluralism, not pluralism celebrated as a public value (which, of course, does not mean that the latter was not tried, especially by early New Labour, which championed Cool Britannia). *Pace* Favell (1997), British multiculturalism is not really a 'philosophy of integration' because it makes no reference to a totality that is the logical prerequisite for 'integration'. Accordingly late New Labour, after having championed multiculturalism as a component feature of a 'rebranded' Britain,[1] found it necessary to move from 'multiculturalism' to 'integration', thus admitting that, whatever 'multiculturalism' was, it was *not* a formula of integration. However, a protagonist of 'bring(ing) the word integration back into fashion' – namely Trevor Phillips, last chairman of the now dissolved Commission for Racial Equality (CRE) – pointed to a problem in the move to integration: '[W]e are all British and we share a common core. *We are going to spend some time looking at what that common core is* (emphasis added).'[2]

Not to know who they are is the distinct problem of the British. This is a problem which, incidentally, popped up in the very rejection of the 'secular fundamentalism' that was seen as driving the French headscarf ban: 'France has become a despotic power, compelling its people to comply with a cruelly defined model of national conduct. Britain [. . .] has a different crisis: We do not know who we are.'[3] Just when *jilbab* and *niqab* came under scrutiny in the judicial sphere, there was a conspicuous scramble for national self-definition in the media and in the political sphere. While the reasons for this extend beyond the headscarf controversy, there was an intrinsic link between rejecting the extreme headscarf and raising the question of identity: if the extreme headscarf was 'such a visible statement of separation and of difference', to reiterate the words of Jack Straw,[4] it had to invite a reflection on the content of the opposite of separation: unity.

One such reflection on national identity, which is representative for many, was conducted by the later Prime Minister Gordon Brown, in his 2004 British Council Annual Lecture.[5] It is an exercise in syllogism that still exposed the pitfalls of British identity, perhaps of any national identity in a liberal society. First, there was the alternative to define national identity either in relation to 'race and ethnicity' or in relation to 'citizenship', and Britain's choice in this matter was obvious: citizenship. Britain shared this disposition with the United States, only the latter had, in addition, a 'mission' which was absent in Britain: 'Indeed we made a virtue of understatement or no statement at all.'[6] But that could not be all, because to 'love our country' had to derive from more than 'occupy[ing] a plot of land': it had to derive from 'values' that were generally valid. In trying to reconcile particularism, without which there could not be a 'strong sense of national identity', and universalism, without which such identity would lapse into ethnicity or race, Brown compiled a list of five British 'values and qualities': liberty, duty, fair play, putting civil society above the state, and an openness to new ideas and influences. Summing it up, Brown defined Britishness as 'a passion for liberty anchored in a sense of duty and an intrinsic commitment to tolerance and fair play'.[7]

The interesting matter is that Brown placed 'liberty' ahead of all other values. Indeed, 'liberty' has been the long-standing common denominator of British *and* English self-definitions – 'liberty was the hallmark of Englishness', writes Linda Colley (1992: 111) in her landmark study on the making of 'Britons'. Even that seeming political opposite of liberty, empire, was defined by it. For Ernest Barker (1951: 8) the British empire was defined by the 'idea of freedom': 'It is, in effect, an empire without *imperium*: an empire which has preferred the opposite principle of *Libertas'*, not without conceding that this was a 'contradiction in terms' and a 'living paradox'.

A national self-definition in terms of liberty raises two problems. First, there is hardly a nation that would not define itself in the same way. Being a universal creed, liberalism effaces national particularism. And, secondly, to the degree that there *is* a national inflection to British liberties, it is one that places private over public values, and this renders it unsuitable as a formula of unity and integration.

Let us further scrutinize the multiculturalism that springs from such roots. Perhaps the prime site for the study of the intrinsic connection between British multiculturalism and liberalism is public education, which – as elsewhere in Europe – has been the main site of the headscarf controversy in Britain. In a perceptive comparison of public education in England, France, and the United States, Meira Levinson (1997) argued that public education in a liberal state is marked by a tension between liberalism, which requires non-interference in the private sphere, and democracy, which, on the contrary, requires public 'character-building', if only for the sake of producing autonomous and emancipated individuals.[8] These opposite requirements are differently realized in different states. Whereas France suppresses the private in favor of the public, England runs to the other extreme, of putting private above public values in public education (the US occupies a middle position, inviting private difference into the public space). In England, this makes for a constellation of 'divided pluralism', in which the public is effectively privatized. Concretely speaking, English education is geared toward 'the effective privatization of nominally public schools' (Levinson 1997: 338, n. 12).

Only reinforced by the 'parental choice' movement under Thatcher and Blair, the subordination of public education to private choice has deep historical roots. According to the 1944 Education Act, which marks the beginning of a state-supervised system of compulsory primary and secondary education in England and Wales, the Anglican and Roman Catholic Churches, which had so far monopolized the education system, retained an important role even after the state take-over. Still today, about one third of all state-financed schools are run by the Church of England or by the Roman Catholic Church. Moreover, as a concession for relinquishing control over education to the state, the churches obtained the favor that *all* schools, the secular ones included, had to provide for compulsory religious education and a daily act of worship. Finally, schools are allowed to discriminate in employment and in student selection on the basis of religion – so that, say, a publicly maintained Catholic school can, in the interest of preserving the 'character of the school', refuse entry to non-Catholic children, irrespective of their talents or achievements (ibid., p. 337). The belated introduction of a national curriculum through the Education Reform Act of 1988 did not do away with the subordination of the public school to the private (religious) sphere. The new subject 'Education for citizenship', for instance, which was meant to instil the public value of British citizenship, remained marginal to the curriculum. The Christian privileges were even enhanced through a mandate that the school prayer had to be of 'a wholly or mainly Christian character' and that religious education had to 'reflect the fact that the religious traditions in Great Britain are in the main Christian' (quoted in Blair and Aps 2005: 2).

What appears blatantly discriminatory, however, was not really so. First, it was always possible to opt out of the religious requirements. Secondly, these requirements could be appropriated by minority religions, with the result of reinforcing the private or group-pandering tilt of English public education. Wherever they formed local majorities – which they often did, because of the highly clustered nature of immigrant settlement in Britain – religious minorities effectively used the local authority structures to mould religious worship and education in their own image, even after the 1988 Education Reform Act (which had been designed precisely as an antidote to this practice). The result was a local focus on Islam or Hinduism; the development of 'multi-faith' syllabuses; and daily assemblies centering on 'the moral aspect that is shared among religions'[9] – which is a euphemism for the turn away from Christianity. Accordingly, there has been 'no strong opposition among Muslims to religious education and no thought that the practice should be abandoned in state-run schools' (Fetzer and Soper, 2005: 41). Most importantly, the quest for 'voluntary aided' or 'voluntary controlled' status, which grants partial or total public funding to private schools, in principle cannot be denied to minority religions. Once the state's financing of private schools was confirmed in the 1988 Education Reform Act, one of the key demands of British Muslim organizations became the creation of their own state-financed schools. After conservative governments had rejected this demand for a long time, arguing that it would fuel segregation, New Labour quickly gave in, and currently there are seven state-financed Muslim schools in England.

The multicultural prolongation of British liberalism, which places private choice over public values, reinforces certain deficiencies of the latter (see Levinson 1997: 340f). Students are not really exposed to difference, as they can withdraw behind the walls of a (quasi-)private school held by 'their' group; no detachment from prior commitments is expected (this pleases especially the Muslims who wish to insulate their offspring from the virus of reflection that is implanted by a secular curriculum); and, overall, there is no public space or body which would be shared by all and which all could identify with. 'Divided pluralism', coined to describe the effect of the British school system, describes quite well British multiculturalism at large: 'a pluralistic national community composed of a number of mutually uninterested mono-religious, mono-cultural, mono-linguistic or mono-economic subcommunities' (p. 340). As Levinson sharply observes, 'multiculturalism' in such a system 'is not treated as a public good' itself; instead 'pluralism is merely an accidental public by-product of a private-regarding school system' (ibid.).

Levinson's diagnosis of 'divided pluralism' resonates with other accounts of British multiculturalism, be they critical or apologetic. On the critical side, Amartya Sen (2006) characterized British multiculturalism as a 'plural monoculturalism', in which 'a diversity of cultures [. . .] might pass one another like ships in the night'. On the apologetic side, Bhikhu Parekh (2001) depicted multicultural Britain as a 'community of communities', though the meta-identity of 'British' is seen as tainted by its 'racialist' connotations. Whether multicultural-ism is denounced or celebrated, if Muslims tap into such structure, how can they not see themselves as a people apart? The video testament of one of the bombers of the London Tube on 7 July 2005, pronounced in a 'measured Yorkshire accent', is an extreme version of this: 'Your democratically elected governments continuously perpetuate atrocities against my people and your support of them makes you directly respon-sible, just as I am directly responsible for protecting and avenging my Muslim brothers and sisters [. . .]'.[10]

A multiculturalism born out of British liberalism blends effortlessly with a state-church regime which notionally privi-leges the Anglican establishment, yet in reality has proved to be highly inclusive of other religions. Like other putatively 'civic' European nationalisms, English and British nationalism has religious roots (see Marx 2003). It was at first conceived of in terms of a 'Protestant Israel' pitted against Catholic France (see Colley 1992: 369) and later on it broadened into a Chris-tian Britain opposed to the atheism of post-revolutionary France, until a generic 'religion' (to be taken as code word for Christianity) was mobilized in the 1944 Education Act against 'pagan' German national socialism (McLeod 1999: 64). As one can see, the religious dimension of Englishness and British-ness was mouldable and broadly inclusive. Britain neverthe-less developed a state-church regime that privileges a specific branch of Christianity: in England and Wales Anglicanism, in Scotland Presbyterianism. Since the 1701 Act of Establish-ment, England's official state church has been the Church of England, the monarch being its supreme governor and 'defender of the faith'. She, together with Parliament, has a say in appointing bishops, twenty-six of whom have ex officio seats in the House of Lords. In characteristically British fashion, where the state is representative of civil society, it was Parliament that determined, in the Act of Establishment, that the monarch had to be Anglican. This demonstrates the reli-gious–nationalist roots of a state–church regime which now sits oddly within a secularized society.

But, again, what appears discriminatory has proved to be highly accommodating of minority religions. Through rules of exception, starting with the Toleration Act (1689) for Protestant dissenters, minority religions were successively incorporated into this arrangement, and lately non-Christian religions also (see König 2003: 95–7). Characteristically, British Muslims are generally not in favor of abolishing the Anglican establishment, even after they lost the battle for being included in a Law on Blasphemy which protects only Christians.[11] This is because 'secularism', the exclusion of religion from public space, is not in their interest. As a British Muslim leader put it: 'For us there must be a church-state link, or rather a religion-state link' (Fetzer and Soper 2005: 60). Instead of wanting to abolish the establishment regime, British Muslim leaders, including intellectuals like Tariq Modood, have advocated taking it into a pluralizing, 'multi-faith' direction. This attempt has had some limited success. Hindus and Muslims can now be found in the House of Lords, not on the basis of a formal quota, but as representatives of their religions nevertheless, and the designated successor to the incumbent monarch, Prince Charles, has long advocated becoming the 'defender of faith' (a move which is naturally rejected by the Christian churches; see Evangelical Alliance 2006: 15). Overall, the British pattern of secularization has been one of 'pluralism' and 'moderation' (Martin 1978: 20f), the state rarely clashing with oppositional religion. The generally smooth and frictionless accommodation of Islam is no exception.[12]

British Muslims, of course, see the matter differently. Their dominant view is one of exclusion and discrimination, even more so than in European states that have been much less accommodating (see Pew Research Center 2006). The logic of this is Tocquevillian: the more a claimant's needs are accommodated, the greater the claimant's appetite for more (see Joppke 2009). A standard complaint of British Muslims since their first appearance as unified claimant during the Rushdie Affair has been that, qua Muslims, they were denied inclusion in the Race Relations Act (RRA), which protects only discrimination 'on racial grounds'. In *Mandla* v. *Dowell Lee* (1983), the House of Lords had famously included Sikhs in this regime, because of their 'racial flavor', so that a school could not exclude a Sikh for wearing a turban which was not part of the school uniform (the case at hand). Similar protection was later denied to Muslims, because they were of 'many nations and colours',[13] and thus not a 'racial group' according to the RRA. All governments since Thatcher refused to amend the Race Relations Act to include religion, fearing to get drawn into the muddy waters of having to distinguish religions from cults,[14] but, above all, of having to approximate religion to race (for the latter, see Hepple and Choudhury 2001: 20).

However, Muslims from predominantly Muslim countries like India, Pakistan, or Bangladesh (home of the vast majority of British Muslims) were always indirectly protected under the Race Relations Act through their 'national origins'. So to be protected *as* Muslim under the RRA was perhaps more a matter of symbolic recognition than of redressing material disadvantage. Moreover, advances in human rights law partially compensated for an unforthcoming anti-discrimination law: since the 1998 Human Rights Act, the European Convention of Human Rights is part of domestic law, and so is, with it, Article 9, which protects religious liberties. Finally, Europe came to a partial rescue even on the anti-discrimination front: since 2003, the EU Employment Directive is a part of British law, granting wide-ranging protection from religious discrimination in the all-important sphere of employment. These European legal advances had interestingly anomalous implications for the later headscarf controversy: pupils, who could invoke 'only' human rights protection, were less protected than teachers, who in addition to human rights law could also invoke the intrinsically stronger anti-discrimination norms of the EU Employment Directive.[15]

Britain's success at accommodating Islam is perhaps best demonstrated in the career of the concept which implies the exact opposite, 'islamophobia'. It was coined in a report of the Runnymede Trust in 1997, which claimed that '[I]n 20 years it [*sc.* islamophobia] has become more explicit, more extreme, more pernicious and more dangerous [. . . It] is part of the fabric of everyday life in modern Britain, in much the same way that anti-Semitic discourse was taken for granted earlier in this century.'[16] This was not the alarmist view of a besieged minority but of a predominantly non-Muslim elite committee which included the Bishop of London, Richard Chartres, and Britain's first female Rabbi, Julia Neuberger; and it was the view of the British Home Minister Jack Straw, who officially launched the report in Parliament. That Britain is 'islamophobic' has since become the dogma the questioning of which is taken to be a proof of its claim – much like questioning the concept of 'racism' is itself 'racist'. Whether 'islamophobia' is real or not, there is a functional need for something akin to it from the point of view of claims-making Muslims. It has grounded the campaign to outlaw religious discrimination analogous to racial discrimination, in that there needed to be a specifically *religious* discrimination if there was to be a specific law and policy against it.

What is 'islamophobia'? The 1997 Runnymede Report defined it as 'closed' views of Islam in which the latter is depicted as 'monolithic', 'separate', or 'inferior' (to cite only the first three out of eight ways of disqualifying Islam) (Commission on British Muslims and Islamophobia 1997). If 'islamophobia' is meant to capture a discrimination against Muslims, it obviously mixes the critique of religious dogma, which is incontrovertible in a liberal society, with quasi-racial prejudice, which, of course, is pernicious. As Kenan Malik (2005) put it aptly, 'the trouble with the idea [of islamophobia] is that it confuses hatred of and discrimination against Muslims on the one hand with criticism of Islam on the other'. In fact, one might well argue that a 'closed' and unchangeable view of Islam is exactly the one that circulates in the quarters that advocate the extreme headscarf. Jytte Klausen (2005: 100), for instance, found that over 70 percent of her British Muslim interviewees (which is the highest percentage among all the European Muslims) espoused a 'neo-orthodox' view of integration, according to which 'the basic tenets of Islam are not for "modification"' and 'Islam is what it is'; so that the idea, germane to political leaders across Europe, of a 'westernized', British, or European Islam is rejected out of hand.

Not just conflating the critique of religious dogma with racial discrimination, the concept of 'islamophobia' also hovers undecidedly between denoting irrational fears (which is the literal meaning of 'phobia') and institutionalized inequalities.

To the degree that it is modeled on anti-semitism and indeed denotes a phobia, 'islamophobia' cannot be decoupled from an actor's intentions or perceptions. However, this sits oddly with the claim, raised in the second Runnymede Report (Commission on British Muslims and Islamophobia 2004: 14), that there is 'institutional islamophobia', defined as 'those established laws, customs and practices which systematically reflect and produce inequalities in society between Muslims and non-Muslims'. The model for this is obviously 'institutional racism', which denotes an objective fact, independent of an actor's intentions or perceptions, built into the anonymous workings of institutions.

Even if one grants the possibility of 'institutional islamophobia', there is not much evidence for it. It is true: British Muslims of Pakistani and Bangladeshi origins are among the poorest, the most highly unemployed, and the worst educated of British minority groups. However, the simple fact that Muslims of Indian and Middle Eastern origins do even better than ordinary Britons in all of these respects casts doubt on the charge that Muslim-specific discrimination is the cause of disadvantage. More likely candidates for this causal role are the average low age of the Pakistani and Bangladeshi populations, the recentness of their arrival, their concentration in economically depressed regions and sectors, and the low level of skills in its first immigrant generation (see Policy Exchange 2007: 68; and Heath and Yu 2005, who argue that low levels of skill trigger sector-specific discrimination). In addition, the low participation of Pakistani and Bangladeshi women in the labor market is also due to internal, cultural-cum-religious factors.[17] Finally, there is evidence, partially due to the heavy concentration of Bangladeshi Muslims in fast-moving London, that the educational gap between them and Indians is rapidly closing, that Bangladeshi women are increasingly leaving home for work, and that even Bangladeshi men 'ditched manual work in droves to go into skilled and professional occupations'.[18]

More than a sensor for discrimination, 'islamophobia' has been the central symbolic device of the British state to recognize its Muslim minority. Jack Straw expressed this openly at the official launching of the first Runnymede Report in the House of Commons: 'This morning's launch provides me personally with a welcome opportunity to state loud and clear the value which the Government places on the Muslim community and our determination to take seriously their concerns. British Muslims bring with them a strong and inspiring history and achievement.'[19] Certifying the existence of 'islamophobia' was the basis for further advances such as including a question on religion in the 2001 census; adding the legal phrase 'religiously aggravated offence' to the Crime and Disorder Act in 2001; and creating the new offence of 'incitement' to religious hatred in the 2006 Racial and Religious Hatred Act (the latter was attacked as a new law on blasphemy by writers, artists and intellectuals who feared for the freedom of speech).

Under the reign of taken-for-granted 'islamophobia', the media and public discourse became permeated by an extreme sense of etiquette and political correctness when dealing with Muslim affairs – giving a lie to the frequent charge that the British media have been a hothouse of islamophobia. In fact, Britain was the only country in Europe which denied its newspaper readers reprints of the drawings of the Prophet that had stirred the so-called Danish Cartoon Affair in 2005. After the London Tube bombings of 7 July 2005, which put the spotlight fully on the domestic sources of Islamic terrorism, a 'moral inversion'[20] led the media to play down the Islamic dimension of the crime, while organized Muslims refused any responsibility and instead deemed themselves victimized by this 'morbid opportunity to attack and undermine British Muslims, their institutions and mosques'.[21]

On the part of media and public institutions, the response to 7/7 was subdued indeed. Not just censoring the notion of an 'Islamic terrorism', BBC even instructed its journalists to avoid the word 'terrorism' when describing the event, and its World Affairs editor referred to the culprits as 'misguided criminals'. This was the position of the police also, whose deputy assistant commissioner stated that 'Islam and terrorists are two words that do not go together'.[22]

Naturally, these were stances dear to the British Muslim leadership. The president of the British Muslim Council, Iqbal

Sacranie, stated that 'there is no such thing as an Islamic terrorist – that is offensive'.[23] In fact, the Muslim response to 7/7 has been, not soul-searching, but a new round of attacking 'islamophobia'. British Muslim leaders issued this statement: 'The tragedy of July 7 demands that all of us confront together the problem of Islamophobia, racism, unemployment and social exclusion – factors that may be alienating some of our children and driving them towards the paths of anger and desperation. The youth needs understanding, not bashing.'[24] Despite the lack of any evidence that the 2005 bombings were followed by a rise in attacks on Muslim women, Zaki Badawi, the usually moderate chairman of the Council of Mosques and Imams, gave out an alarmist 'fatwa' that 'Muslim women who fear being attacked physically or verbally [. . .] remove their *hijab* so as not to be identified by those who are hostile to Muslims'.[25]

The Extreme Headscarf in British Courts

It is no wonder that the first protagonist in Britain's unfolding headscarf controversy, Shabina Begum, depicted herself as a victim of islamophobia: 'As a young woman growing up in post-9/11 Britain, I have witnessed a great deal of bigotry from the media, politicians and legal officials.' One wonders: which media, which politicians, which officials? This is a quintessentially British statement which would be inconceivable in France or Germany, countries with distinctly less etiquette when dealing with Muslim claims. A heterodox Muslim pundit crisply articulated the underlying logic: 'Paradoxically, telling Muslims that they are vulnerable and need to be "listened" to has only made them feel more like outsiders who cannot be expected to handle criticism like everyone else.'[26]

The essentials of the Begum case, which kicked off the British headscarf controversy, are well-known (a detailed legal account is to be found in McGoldrick 2006, ch. 6). Born in 1988 and of Pakistani origins, Shabina Begum was a student of Denbigh High School in Luton, Bedfordshire. Until September 2002, she 'happily wore her *shalwar kameeze*',[27] a loose-fitting tunic and trousers worn with a headscarf – which is the widely used religious alternative to the school uniform among female South Asian minority pupils, including Sikhs and Hindus.[28] On the first day of the new school year, 3 September 2002, she arrived dressed in what appeared to the assistant head teacher as a 'long skirt' – a *jilbab*.[29] She was accompanied by her brother (suspected to be close to the radical Hizb ut-Tahrir), who 'talked of human rights and legal proceedings', in a 'forceful' tone that appeared 'unreasonable as it verged on the threatening'. The assistant head teacher told Shabina to go home and 'return to school wearing correct school uniform'. This she did not. Instead, she fought her case through all legal instances, including the House of Lords.

The *jilbab* (and its usual complement, the *niqab*) is unknown to the South Asian Hanafi school of Islam, which is moderate in its prescriptions of religious dress. Instead, the extreme headscarf originates in the Saudi Arabian Hambali school of Islam, which is the only one of the four Sunni schools pre-scribing it for women from puberty on.[30] In Britain, it is propa-gated by radical groups surrounding the Hizb ut-Tahrir, and no more than a tiny (though 'increasing') fraction (10,000–40,000) out of the 800,000 British Muslim women is believed to be wearing it.[31]

Obviously a foreign and recent import on Britain's predomi-nantly South Asian Muslim scene, the *jilbab* and the *niqab* entered an already thoroughly pluralized school setting. Like many schools in Britain, Denbigh High School 'has bent over backwards to satisfy all reasonable and proper religious require-ments'.[32] This was a school frequented to almost 80 percent by Muslim pupils and accommodating a total of forty lan-guages and twenty-one ethnic groups. Minorities were the majority here. The head teacher was a Bengali Muslim who had grown up in South Asia, and four of the six parent gover-nors were Muslim, as were three of the governors externally appointed by the Local Education Authority (LEA). With the participation and approval of Muslim parents and of local mosques, the school had devised a new uniform in 1993, which included the possibility of *shalwar kameeze* in the right school colors for Muslim girls. Consented by all, the school uniform was said to have 'promoted a positive ethos and a sense of communal identity' among pupils.[33] Under her Bengali headteacher, Denbigh High School had also excelled academically, with performance results that were 'well above average for schools with a similar intake'.[34] This is why Shabina, who lived outside the school's catchment area, *chose* to attend it (there were three schools in the same area which all tolerated the *jilbab* and which she could have attended instead). In sum, this was a rather multicultural and permissive setting for a headscarf controversy to appear.

The Begum case was one of the first test cases for the 1998 Human Rights Act, which came into force in October 2000, incorporating into domestic law the 1950 European Convention for the Protection of Human Rights and Fundamental Freedoms (henceforth ECHR). For the first time Britain had something akin to a constitutional rights charter that could be invoked by any individual against the state, which had long been a reality on the European Continent. Article 9. 1 of the ECHR protects the 'freedom [. . .] in public or private, to manifest [one's] religion' – subject only to 'public order' and 'public safety' considerations and the 'rights and freedom of others' (Article 9. 2). The question now was whether Shabina's right to her own religion had been violated by 'excluding' her from school for wearing the *jilbab*. In the first instance ruling in this case, the High Court denied that an Article 9. 1 violation had occurred. In its view (criticized as 'not so convincing' by McGoldrick 2006: 182), Shabina had been excluded only for refusing to respect the school uniform policy, not for her religious beliefs. The court cited the possibility to wear the *shalwar kameeze* as an alternative to the school uniform, which the local Muslim authorities consulted in this case considered to be 'fulfil[ling] the requirements of Islamic dressing'.[35] Overall, the school uniform policy 'pursued a legitimate aim and was proportionate', and the limitations exacted on the religious liberties of some were necessary 'for the protection of the rights and freedoms of others'. The court referred in this respect to other Muslim girls, who might 'feel pressure on them' to wear the *jilbab* if it were allowed.[36]

Interestingly, the 'public order' constraint, which is *also* available in the Article 9. 2 restriction of religious freedom and would allow the latter to be restricted for the sake of public values such as 'social cohesion and harmony amongst the pupils', was mentioned by the court only in passing. In putting the onus on third-party rights, the school was projected primarily as a private space, and it also came 'dangerously close to allowing individuals to be judged by the prejudices of others', as a legal commentator criticized the court decision (Davies 2005: 520).

However, 'Shabina Begum' became a household formula only after the Court of Appeal, rather spectacularly, repealed the High Court decision, in a rule on 2 March 2005.[37] This was particularly unexpected, as the European Court of Human Rights (ECtHR) in Strasbourg had just decided, in *Sahin* v. *Turkey*, that a Turkish university policy prohibiting the wearing of Islamic headscarves was not contrary to Article 9 of the ECPHR, because governments had a wide 'margin of appreciation' to decide on a matter sensitive to the 'rights and freedom of others' and to the 'maintenance of public order'.[38] *Sahin* v. *Turkey* only confirmed a conservative streak of Strasbourg jurisprudence on the Islamic headscarf, so that 'Europe' was unlikely ever to come to the rescue, once domestic instances had failed to provide a remedy.

The Court of Appeal brushed off the European Court rule on Sahin with the strange argument that Britain was 'not a secular state', so that other standards (one wonders: those of a religious state?) would have to apply.[39] Arguing that Denbigh High School *had* 'excluded' Shabina for 'manifest[ing] her religion', the Court of Appeal held that an Article 9 violation *had* occurred. However, the gist of the judgment was not on the substance but on the procedure of the exclusion. There may have been good reasons for the school to override the plaintiff's religious freedom, only the school had not followed the proper procedure in doing so: '[I]t was for the school, as an emanation of the state, to justify the limitation on her freedom created by the school's uniform code [. . .] The school had not approached the matter in that way. It had started from the premise that its uniform policy was there to be obeyed [. . . I]t [. . .] had not attributed to the claimant's beliefs the weight that they deserved.'[40]

A legal critic condemned the Court of Appeal's 'procedural' approach as a 'recipe for judicialisation on an unprecedented scale' (Poole 2005: 695). On this view, the 'proportionality' test was an *ex post facto* test, to be applied by judges only; it was not a test to be used by public authorities ahead of their decision-making. A more appreciating observer, who deemed the Court of Appeal ruleing on Begum 'good news for rights', still conceded that it was at odds with the 'almost anti-procedural' ECtHR jurisprudence (Davies 2005: 516f). On the other hand, what is a 'right' if it is not recognized as such in everyday life? As two legal commentators pointed out, school administrators are expected 'to understand [. . .] a mass of legal rules, from employment law, to health and safety regulations to school discipline' (Carney and Sinclair 2006: 137). Then why not expect them to be cognizant of fundamental human rights precepts in the school context? One sees that Britain, which had long resisted the trend towards continental-style constitutional politics, has now fully succumbed to it.

However, the last word in the Begum case was with the House of Lords. On 22 March 2006, the Law Lords overruled the Court of Appeal and reinstated the High Court view that Shabina had been rightfully excluded for her violation of the school uniform policy.[41] The 'procedural approach' of the Court of Appeal was thrown out: this was 'admirable guidance to a lower court [. . .] but cannot be required of a headteacher'.[42] In substantive regard, the Law Lords argued in two steps. First, there had been no violation of Shabina's Article 9 right to religion, because the article 'does not require that one should be allowed to manifest one's religion at any time and place of one's own choosing'.[43] Now it became relevant that there were three schools nearby which tolerated the *jilbab*, and that Shabina could have attended one of them instead. This reasoning explicitly realigned British jurisprudence with the 'margin of appreciation' approach of the European Court of Human Rights, which likewise held that no interference with a religious right existed if religious beliefs could be practised elsewhere or despite the state's restriction (see Carney and Sinclair 2005: 133). In a second step, the Law Lords held that, even if a violation of an Article 9 right had existed in this case, it was still overridden by the school's uniform policy, which was 'objectively justified'. Anxious to identify an explicit Article 9. 2 constraint, the Law Lords pointed again to the school uniform's function of protecting the rights of non-*jilbab* wearing Muslim girls, much as the first-instance court had done before, only that the evidence for the violation of these rights had even increased in the meantime.[44]

As in the High Court, the majority Law Lords' reference to third-party rights was purely one in terms of private choice, thus reinforcing the private tilt of British public schooling. Only Baroness Hale went further. She argued in French style that schools should give Muslim girls the opportunity to develop the personal autonomy they could not acquire at home: 'Like it or not, this is a society committed, in principle and in law, to equal freedom for men and women to choose how they will lead their lives within the law. Young girls from ethnic, cultural or religious minorities growing up here face particularly difficult choices: how far to adopt or to distance themselves from the dominant culture. A good school will enable and support them.'[45] This was the only intervention in the Begum case which invoked gender equality as an argument against the extreme headscarf.

Overall, the Begum case, despite its dramatic twists and turns as it moved up the legal instances, did not question the fundamental British *démarche* in dealing with the Islamic headscarf: that this was a matter best decided at local level by the respective school. The Law Lords even couched this approach as deference towards Parliament, which had allowed schools to decide on school uniforms in the absence of a national policy.[46] This response reinstated the typically British hands-off approach of the judiciary vis-à-vis the state. As Lord Bingham described the gist of the House of Lords decision at the outset, it 'concerns a particular pupil and a particular school in a particular place and at a particular time [. . .] The House [of Lords] is not, and could not be, invited to rule whether Islamic dress, or any feature of Islamic dress, should or should not be permitted in the schools of this country.'[47]

The political import of the Begum saga thus remained limited. Politicians rarely commented on the case. Prime

Minister Blair, whose wife, Cherie Booth, happened to be Begum's barrister in the Court of Appeal and in the House of Lords, long stuck to the line that the Islamic headscarf was a matter of 'individual choice' and not something for the government to have an opinion on, let alone to decide about.[48]

This changed when the face veil, the *niqab*, moved into the picture. Now the headscarf was no longer just a matter of 'individual choice', on which local schools or judges – at the most – might have a say. Instead it became a matter of national unity and integration, a concern for all. This change of tone is epitomized by Jack Straw's much-publicized insistence that Muslim women should take off their *niqab* in his Blackburn constituency bureau.[49] Straw brought two new themes into the debate. First, he raised the sociolinguistic (or, with respect to the veil, instrumental) issue that a face-to-face communication was diminished by being unable to '– almost literally – see what the other person means'. Secondly, from a political angle the face veil was a 'visible statement of separation and of difference' which marked the limit of toleration in a liberal society. Both of these themes were subsequently pursued in two different arenas: politicians and public intellectuals struggled over the *niqab* as a 'mark of separation', and even Prime Minister Blair came around to indicting it.[50] In the legal arena, the question was whether a *niqab*, on the part of teachers and pupils alike, would stand in the way of effective classroom communication and thus obstruct the school's function of disseminating knowledge.

The *niqab* first became an issue when a young assistant teacher, Aishah Azmi, was suspended by her school after suddenly insisting on covering her face in the classroom. From 2005, Mrs Azmi had been employed part-time, by a state-controlled Church of England school as a bilingual support worker. This was a junior school for seven to eleven-year-olds, 90 percent of whom were Muslim and ethnic minority (mostly Indian and Pakistani). Azmi was employed especially to support the learning and welfare of ethnic minority pupils. A 'devout Muslim', Azmi had worn the face veil in the presence of unrelated adult males since she was sixteen. However, when interviewed for the job, Azmi wore a simple headscarf that left her face uncovered. In her first week of work, Azmi insisted on putting on the face veil when teaching together with males. The headteacher refused to accept this, with the instrumental argument that the 'veil reduced her effectiveness.' The school eventually suspended Azmi for her refusal to unveil 'whilst working with children'.[51]

Like Begum, 'Azmi' immediately turned into a court case. However, as it involved a private employment contract, the legal framework differed – it was a matter of anti-discrimination law, within the ambit of the EU 2000 Employment Directive (domestically incorporated in terms of the Employment Equality [Religion or Belief] Regulations 2003), to be dealt with by an employment tribunal. On 6 October 2006, the Employment Tribunal in Leeds rejected three of Azmi's four claims of 'direct' and 'indirect discrimination', 'harassment' and 'victimization' on grounds of her religion.[52] Only a minor claim of 'victimization' was left standing. The judgment made reference to diminished effectiveness when teaching behind a veil, and it quoted approvingly the direct observations of the head teacher: '[I]t was readily apparent that the children she [sc. Azmi] was working with were seeking visual clues from her which they could not obtain because they could not see her facial expressions.'[53] Advice sought earlier by the school from the Education Service amounted to the same: 'Obscuring the face and mouth reduces the non-verbal signals required between adult and pupil [. . .] A pupil needs to see the adult's full face in order to receive optimum communication.'[54] In fact, the instruction pack to new teachers, which Mrs Azmi had received during her training, said in reference to children learning a second language: '[G]esture and body language, including facial expression, reinforce the spoken word.'[55]

The Employment Tribunal's October 2006 decision on Azmi, which was upheld in the Employment Appeal Tribunal in March 2007,[56] also gives good insight into the practical workings of anti-discrimination law. The charge of direct discrimination required a 'comparator', that is, a person who is not Muslim and who covered her face ('perhaps following a head or facial injury with bandages'[57]) but was *not* sanctioned. As Mrs Azmi failed to show that she was treated less favorably than such 'comparator', the charge of direct discrimination was dismissed. With respect to indirect discrimination, the question was whether there was a 'provision, criterion or practice' (PCP) applied by the school which was 'apparently neutral' but which put Mrs Azmi at a 'particular disadvantage' because of her religion *and* which was not justified by a 'legitimate aim' and achieved by 'appropriate means'. Because the Employment Tribunal deemed this potentially to be the case, the question was whether the PCP was legitimate in aim and appropriate in means. The *legitimacy in aim* was established by the obvious 'need for these particular pupils to be able to see the teacher's face and observe the way in which her mouth framed the words of the English language'.[58] With respect to the *appropriateness of means*, the suspension was issued only after a protracted trial period of six months. A written notice to unveil was given as late as November 2006, some two months into the conflict, after the evidence for reduced effectiveness when teaching behind a veil had been established. And the order to unveil applied only to the context of the classroom, so that Mrs Azmi was free to 'wear her veil at all other times, and in particular when she was moving to different parts of the school'.[59] In fact, in a letter sent to the head teacher on 12 December 2006, Mrs Azmi felt 'very appreciative of all your help and understanding' and she fathomed that 'it is not your intention to place any undue stress on me'.[60] One is therefore surprised how four days earlier Mrs Azmi could have filed in a grievance 'about the manner in which I have been discriminated against in regards to wearing my veil due to my religious belief', which started the legal procedure.[61] The Azmi case is a testimonial to the utmost sense of protocol in which even the most delicate Muslim claims have been handled in Britain.

In the (so far) final intervention of British courts on the extreme headscarf, the *niqab* became an issue for pupils also.[62] As in the Azmi case, the instrumental argument that the *niqab* stood in the way of effective classroom communication fared again prominently. The case concerned a twelve-year-old Muslim girl (referred to in High Court as 'X'), who in her second year of study in a selective all-girls grammar school insisted on wearing a *niqab*. As her three sisters had previously attended the same school, all with a *niqab*, 'X' raised, in addition to the usual ECHR Article 9 claim, two further 'legitimate expectation' and 'similar treatment' claims, which essentially asked for her to be treated as her sisters had been. Even less than in the Begum case could one say that this was a case of inescapable hardship for one's religious belief: as the case unfolded in court, 'X' was offered a place at another selective girls' grammar school that allowed the *niqab*, along with free transport by the local authority. But she refused the offer. And, as in the Begum case, the case of 'X' occurred in a school which had already made ample provision for alternative religious dress – so much so that even a Muslim advocacy group, the Muslim Educational Centre of Oxford, deemed that 'this is multiculturalism gone too far',[63] offering the school to cover some of the legal costs (which the school rejected). However frivolous the claim may have been, considering a legal bill that could reach £500,000, this was a case which threatened to drive the school into financial ruin, and a fearful Buckinghamshire County Council promptly backed off from funding the legal procedure.[64]

In its dismissal of the Article 9 claim from the *niqab* pupil, the High Court approvingly cited the reasons adduced by the head teacher for prohibiting the *niqab*. At the top of a list which included reference to the school uniform's promotion of 'uniformity', 'security', and 'avoid[ance of] pressure' on other Muslim girls, there was a concern about 'educational factors'[65]. This meant, much like in the Azmi case, that 'effective classroom interaction' hinged on being unveiled, now also on the part of pupils. The head teacher explained: '[B]eing able to see facial expressions is a key component of effective classroom interaction. Successful teaching depends on the teacher being able "to read" a student to see if the student understands, is paying attention, is distressed, or is enthusiastic.'[66] This 'educational factor' was deemed especially relevant as English was not the first language of 'X' and as she was 'so very quiet and shy' that she had already been subjected to a special education plan before starting to wear the *niqab*.

In rejecting the 'legitimate expectation' and 'similar treatment' claims of 'X', the High Court also reaffirmed the central British *démarche* on the Islamic headscarf, which was not altered in any way by the case rulings from Begum to Azmi to 'X': namely that there was 'substantial margin of discretion' on the part of head teachers to set or change course as they deemed 'required in this school in this town at this time',[67] though on the high floor of already established, and never revoked, multicultural accommodation.

'Marker of Separation': the Political Opposition to the Extreme Headscarf

If the *niqab* became scrutinized in court for its instrumental aspect of hindering communication, politicians and public intellectuals branded it as a 'marker of separation', to reiterate the words of Prime Minister Blair. Only now the conflict expanded from the legal into the political sphere proper, and Britain had a fully fledged headscarf controversy. Since the 2001 race unrest in northern England, which was reinforced by the rise of home-grown Islamic terrorism, there had been concerns about British Muslims' tendency to lead 'parallel lives', separate from mainstream society (see Cantle Report 2001). No better expression for this than the *niqab* – it stood for 'voluntary apartheid'.[68] The *niqab* was perceived as destructive of an elementary human reciprocity. The *niqab* 'rejects human communalities', finds Britain's leading Muslim columnist; 'the women can observe their fellow citizens but remain unseen, like CCTV cameras. They dehumanize themselves and us.'[69]

How should one respond to the veil? asks a *Guardian* man. 'Is it saying, "Don't look at me", or "Look at me"?'[70] One *niqab* wearer, a thirty-five-year-old medical professional who had adopted it after receiving 'guidance from God' at an Islamic conference in Leicester, has the answer: 'No one was staring at me. I know how I felt – like a pearl in an oyster shell, totally protected. No one will step up to you when you are dressed like this.'[71] But to refuse to be 'just like bait for the men'[72], wasn't this another way of defining women solely by their sexuality? 'In truth, half-naked women and veiled women are both solely defined by sexuality', finds Yasmin Alibhai-Brown.[73]

And it was the veiled variant that was even worse for women, as it was a 'physical manifestation of the pernicious idea of women as carriers of Original Sin, whose faces or hair turn Muslim men into predators' – unveiled women 'ask for rape', as Alibhai-Brown quotes a Danish Mufti.[74]

Through denying it, the *niqab* also threw light on the line dividing the private from the public, even in a Britain that has a rather understated sense of the public: 'What any of us does in our own lives is a private matter [. . .] But once we enter the job market or national and local authority domains [. . .] privacy and individual choice become contested quite rightly, for there is such a thing as British society.'[75]

The *niqab* made Britain almost appear like France. 'Almost', because the floor of multiculturalism was rarely put into question: 'No one I know objects to a Muslim headscarf. But as for all the other restrictive clothing, I just don't like seeing them on British streets': this was a typical response.[76] If the 'Muslim community' closed ranks behind the veil, arguing that '[t]oday the veil, tomorrow it could be the beard, *jilbab* and thereafter the head-scarf', this was rational from the point of view of political mobilization. But it was unduly alarmist because no one, not even in the allegedly 'ruthless' media, ever put the simple headscarf to disposition. Moreover, to argue that the veil (in the narrow sense) 'is an Islamic practice and not a cultural or a customary one' and thus 'not open to debate' was a fundamentalist position, but not the one shared by 'the consensus of Muslim scholars'.[77]

While politicians, pundits, and Muslim leaders talked their talk, there were practical responses, as well as more problems on the ground. Imperial College London imposed a *niqab* ban on its students for security reasons. The Council of Heads of Medical Schools decreed: 'Covering the face while meeting a patient is unacceptable as it breaches the duty to make care of the patient your first concern.' Birmingham University School of Medicine promptly banned the veil in lectures and around the campus.[78] More on the farcical side, the Driving Standards Agency (DSA) ordered female test examiners to remove the face veil discreetly from Muslim women, in a private room with a female chaperone or interpreter. This was after some

500 reported cases of fraudulent 'impersonations'.[79] Less farci-
cally, suicide bombers in Iraq and Afghanistan had long used
the veil as a cover for their business. Britain got a taste of the
veil's security implications when the prime suspect in the
killing of a policewoman, the Somali Mustaf Jama, fled Britain
behind a *niqab* using his sister's passport, even though at the
time he was Britain's most wanted criminal and even though
Heathrow Airport, from where he escaped, was in a state of
high alert after the bombings of July 2005.[80] There was a true
cascading of the many problems: ethical, professional, safety-
related, that all emanated from the veil's asymmetry of letting
its wearer see without being seen.

The government response still remained limited to the
domain where the extreme headscarf had first emerged: education. And it responded in a way that reaffirmed the school's
discretion in dealing with the veil. The new 'Guidance to
schools on school uniform related policies', issued by the
Department for Education and Skills (DfES) immediately
after the High Court 2007 decision on the pupil's *niqab*,[81] still
included an important novelty: for the first time, conditions
were specified under which schools were encouraged to ban
the veil. One has to realize that, since the Race Relations
Amendment Act of 2000, schools, like all public authorities,
were mandated to have a 'racial equality scheme', which forced
them to be extra-alert in matters of school uniform. Concretely, 'no pupil should be disciplined for no-compliance with
a uniform policy that results from them having to adhere to a
particular cultural, racial or religious dress code'.[82] While this
line was notionally retained, the 2007 DfES guidance stipulated that the 'freedom to manifest a religion' was not absolute
but could be restricted for reasons of 'health, safety and the
protection of the rights and freedoms of others'. As the guidance admits, this was a line 'confirmed in two recent court
cases': the High Court decisions on Begum and on 'X'. In
the end, the extreme headscarf was reined in by the British
judiciary. This sets an interesting counterpoint to the situation
in France and Germany, where headscarf restrictions origi-
nated from the political branches of the state against rights-
protecting courts.

5 Liberalism and Muslim Integration

Each European country considered in this study had the headscarf controversy it deserved: passionately political and philosophical in France, legalistic to crypto-nationalist in Germany, sanely understated to bizarrely extremist in Britain. But each country, despite highly divergent legacies of state, religion and nationhood, still *had* a headscarf controversy. So isn't there something commonly *European* in this?

Ever since 2001, there has been much scrutiny of the paradox that only Europe, but not the United States, the 'great Satan' of radical Islamism, has problems in integrating Muslim immigrants.[1] For one American observer (Fukuyama 2006: 14), the reason is that 'national identities in Europe remain far more blood-and-soil based' and less 'political' than in the United States. This is an obvious non-starter for 'republican' France and 'multicultural' Britain; even for 'Christian–occidental' Germany, where is the blood, where is the soil? For another American commentator, Europe's troubles with Muslims reveal it to be a 'closed Christian club'.[2] Again: is this Britain, is this France? The same question has to be asked of Aristide Zolberg and Long Litt Woon (1999: 7), who similarly referred Europe's problem of Muslim integration to the fact that 'European identity [. . .] remains deeply embedded in Christian tradition'. If that were the case, why has the institutionally most 'Christian' of our cases, Britain, whose head of state is the 'defender of the faith', also been the most accommodative of Muslims, and not only with respect to the headscarf (see Joppke 2009)? And the (so far) last in a string of American commentary on the European Muslim problem, Joan Scott (2007), in a nuanced and elegant account of the

French headscarf controversy which is laudably sensitive to 'local context' and eschews lump-talk of a 'European' Muslim problem (p. 9), finds that a colonial view of Muslims as 'lesser people' undergirds the French aversion to the headscarf. In her view, the 'fervent nationalism' of the champions of laicity is really 'another mark for racism' (p. 98).

Various accents are set throughout these analyses: nationalism, racism, exclusive state-church amalgams. But always the culprit is 'Europe' and an alleged exclusiveness of its states, cultures, and peoples. And one can hear loud and clear the sigh of relief – luckily not here, in America, where the 'recognition of difference' is in place (Scott 2007: 182).

The attentive reader of this book will have difficulties identifying a common 'European' theme along such lines. If anything, Europe's problems with Muslim integration seem to be more on the input-side: Muslims' vast over-representation in the immigrant population, their low levels of skill and education, and their persistent socio-economic marginalization, even into the second and third immigrant generations. There is no evidence that religious exclusion is behind these integration deficits. Being 'Muslim' in a credal sense is not the source of disadvantage. Instead, religion is the globally available idiom to articulate other-caused disadvantage.

Schirin Amir-Moazami (2007) sharply observed, in a study of France and Germany, that headscarf controversies are a second-generation phenomenon and that 'looking closely, they coincide with the institutionalization of Islam' (p. 15). In other words, 'Islam' is peripheral to the problems of Muslim integration in Europe. The fixation on headscarf controversies, to which, of course, a book on headscarves must contribute, is doubly distorting. First, it highlights an *exception* to the rule of successful accommodation of Islam in Europe, both through the individual rights and through the organizational recognition tracks. If one considers that explicit *Muslim* claims did not emerge in earnest before 1989, the year of the Rushdie controversy in Britain and of the first Foulard Affair in France, the speed and depth of accommodating Muslims have been breathtaking, up to the point that 'laicist' France is now providing state-financed Imam education[3]. Secondly, in conveying that religion is the problem, a headscarf fixation distracts from the real causes of disadvantage, which are mainly socio-economic. To the limited degree that religion contributes to Muslims' socio-economic problems, it does so less as a cause of discrimination than as a repository of Islamic precepts preventing women from seeking employment outside the family. In Britain, for instance, this is considered the 'main reason' why Pakistani and Bangladeshi Muslims 'remain at the bottom of the economic pile'.[4]

By the same token, it is simply not true, as Joan Scott (2007) claims in the case of France, that the law-makers' fixation on banning the headscarf was meant to *deny* existing socio-economic disadvantage, being 'a delusional "fix" given the much larger set of social problems that needed to be addressed' (p. 115). Instead, there has been a lexical ordering of tackling the headscarf first and fighting discrimination next. The Stasi Report (2003: section 3. 3. 1) was well aware of epidemic unemployment and school failure in the *cités*, and there was no presumption that banning the headscarf would be a remedy to this. On the contrary, as if driven by guilt, French law-makers stressed that a headscarf ban would have to be 'accompanied by a more marked effort to combat all discriminations'.[5] Epitomized by the creation of the Haute Autorité de lutte contre les discriminations et pour l'égalité (HALDE) in early 2005, the 'combat' against discrimination promptly took off just when the headscarf chapter was considered closed.

More philosophically attuned than their European neighbors, the French picked up on the affront to liberalism that the headscarf and the entire challenge of Islam constituted. If anything, *this* is the common European theme underlying the headscarf struggles reviewed in this book, even though it is one that is only obliquely 'European'.[6] This dimension is strikingly left out by Joan Scott, who reduces to parochial 'French republican theory' the view that 'the autonomous individual [. . .] exists prior to his or her choices of lifestyle, values, and politics' (2007: 127). This may be 'French republican theory', but it is liberal theory, too – Rawls' 'original position' and his notion of 'public reason', according to which one should address one's fellow citizens only in non-sectarian terms that *all* can understand, is premised on the exact same view of the individual. Conversely, the Islamic view of the individual as 'self-governing but not autonomous' (Talal Asad, quoted ibid., 128) cannot but clash with the liberal view. It is unhelpful to deny this clash of principles under the label of 'racism'. So is an alternative way of denying the conflict through a strangely elastic definition of 'autonomy', according to which the latter is not, as one would think, 'rejecting the pressures of religion and family' but, weirdly, 'understanding the choices others have urged you to make' (Scott 2007: 104). If this is autonomy, what is submission?

If the freely chosen veil, thriving on an individualized, de-ethnicized understanding of Islam (see Roy 2004, ch. 4), is the biggest casualty of anti-headscarf laws, one also has to see that the choice exhibited in donning it is truncated. If the veil is chosen, this is a choice which immediately denies itself. Because, if the veil were a matter of choice all the way down, why not take it off according to the moment? Instead, head-scarf women say they have no choice because God has chosen for them. But how can having no choice be a choice? A study of headscarf-wearing women in Germany and France, which set out to find traces of 'Islamic feminism' and of criticizing Islam 'from within', found mostly views that reaffirmed 'orthodox Islamic discourse', which notably 'disadvantage[s] women' (Jouili and Amir-Moazami 2006: 633f). Strikingly similar to the 'pious' women of the Egyptian mosque move-ment (Mahmood 2005), the knowledge-driven, and thus non-traditionalist, French and German Muslim women's search for the 'pure Islam' only reinvented the traditionalist wisdom that ' "submission" and "obedience" can manifest Islamic virtues' (Jouili and Amir-Moazami 2006: 634). As a French mosque activist explains her vision of the 'pious self': 'The conscious and rigorous Muslim who loves Allah and who wants to satisfy him is more in the domain of duty [. . .] than in the domain of rights.' Who would quarrel with calling this 'a new form of submission' (p. 638)?

If individualized Islam remains under the spell of Islamic orthodoxy, the former cannot but reinforce the orthodox tenet that the Koran is 'uncreated' and co-eternal with God. This is because something akin to the Second Vatican Council, in which the Catholic Church belatedly accepted historical criticism of the Bible, has yet to occur in Islam. The intellectual groundwork for reform may exist (as is claimed by Roy 2005: 80–8 and astutely exercised for a western audience by Barlas 2002), but not the 'leadership through which reformist ideas can be effected at the popular level' (Ruthven 2007: 8). If fundamentalism was originally defined by the belief in the 'inerrancy' of the Bible, Islam, which in all its shades attributes to the Koran a similarly infallible status, is structurally fundamentalist. Samuel Huntington (1996: 217) has got it right: 'The underlying problem for the West is not Islamic fundamentalism. It is Islam.' In pious Muslims there reverberates the archaic power of religion, which is not merely subjective belief, as which it is processed in the liberal constitutional state, but objective truth, which cannot leave room for choice. Accordingly, as Nomi Stolzenberg (1993: 612) demonstrated in a brilliant analysis of the US Supreme Court's famous Mozert case, even 'neutrality' is an assault to religious beliefs, as it brackets the question of their truth.

Jürgen Habermas (2006: 14) argued that the 'religious citizen' in the West is expected to be able to take three 'epistemic attitudes': first, towards 'other religions', thus accepting religious pluralism; secondly, towards 'the independence of secular from sacred knowledge', thus accepting modern science; and, thirdly, towards 'the priority that secular reasons enjoy in the political arena', thus accepting positive law and profane morality. Islam provides obstacles in all three respects, because it presents itself as the final revelation which supersedes Judeo-Christianity (and thus cannot but look down on the latter, even though much less so than on the much inferior non-Abrahamic religions), and because it rejects the cognitive and moral dualisms that are the hallmark of western Christianity.

It is even difficult to retain the distinction, dear to polite opinion in the West, between Islam as religion and 'Islamism' as politicized religion (in this sense, see International Crisis Group 2005). Islam is not a 'religion of peace', as US President George Bush and others want it to be,[7] but a 'religion of law', which is 'inherently concerned with governance and so political in tendency' (ibid., p. 2). As Hans Küng (2004: 115) noted, 'theology' as reflection about God is only of 'secondary importance' in Islam. Instead, 'religious law' is the paramount preoccupation. Even for ordinary Muslims, 'Islam is an intrinsically public matter' (International Crisis Group 2005: 2), not to be limited to a merely private sphere. The International Crisis Group provocatively concludes that the 'postulated antithesis between "ordinary Muslims" and Islamic activists is flimsy and liable to break down under pressure. And it can safely be said that most, if not all, Muslim populations today are living under great pressure' (ibid.).

A closer look at how mainstream Muslim jurists view the presence of Muslim immigrants in the West confirms the intrinsically political nature of Islam (see Shavit 2007). While Muslim jurists no longer object to Muslims' immigration to the West, this is on the condition that they 'place religious identity above national and ethnic identities and [. . .] promote the interests of a global Muslim nation' and that they excel as 'model Muslim[s]' (p. 2). If Joan Scott saw the French head-scarf ban as being motivated by the (questionable) view that 'one could not be both Muslim and French' (2007: 135), one should be aware that this view, however little water it may hold in France, is exactly reciprocated by leading Muslim jurists such as the Egyptian Yusuf al-Qaradawi, the head of the European Council for Fatwa and Research, who is considered by many as 'the most powerful theologian of the Islamic world'.[8]

In particular, three religious duties are imposed on Muslim immigrants. First, they have to be united, 'like a building whose bricks cement each other' (Qaradawi, quoted in Shavit 2007: 2). Secondly, they have to resist assimilation. In particular, if Muslims 'find it extremely difficult to bring up their children as Muslims, they should return to their countries of origin' (Qaradawi, ibid., p. 4). Finally, they have to proselytize. Says Qaradawi: 'Muslims in the West should be sincere callers to their religion. They should keep up in mind that calling others to Islam is not only restricted to scholars and sheikhs, but it goes far to encompass every committed Muslim' (p. 5).

If the French Conseil d'Etat, in its famous 1989 *avis*, denied that the headscarf was in itself proselytizing, Qaradawi would respond that a non-proselytizing headscarf wearer had failed in her religious obligation. In sum, immigration is okayed, even welcomed as a 'powerful weapon in the struggle between the West and Islam' (p. 3), but only on the condition of heightened religious vigilance and activism. While western political elites worry about the Muslims' 'dual loyalty', this is no issue for Muslim jurists, for whom western nation–states are 'mere social mechanisms enabling Muslims to practice Islam to its fullness' (ibid. 6). Expected to implode from their inner spiritual void, if not to be destroyed by the wrath of God for their 'idolatrous barbarism' (Buruma and Margalit 2004: 102), western nation–states are simply no serious competitor to the spiritually strong, global Muslim nation. As Uriya Shavit (2007: 6) sums it up in her unsparing review: 'For mainstream Muslim jurists, Islam is not a culture, a religion, or a tradition, but rather an alternative type of nationality which claims jurisdiction over all aspects of human activities.'

For Islamic doctrine, the Muslim immigrants' 'integration' into the western nation–state is at best instrumental. A good example for this is the 'Islamic Charter' of the Central Council of Muslims in Germany (CCMG), issued in February 2002, with much fanfare, to clarify 'the relation of Muslims to state and society'.[9] Its Sections 10 to 13 indeed commit the 'Muslims living in Germany' (the notion of 'German Muslims', dear to German politicians of all stripes, is carefully avoided) to the principles of the Basic Law, and to renouncing the goal of 'creating a clerical theocratic state'. But these sections have to be read 'with the eyes of a religious jurist and his sense for small print', as one cognoscente advises (Ammann 2004: 84). The commitment to secular law is conditional on the notion that being granted a visa, residence permit, or naturalization are 'contracts' which oblige the Muslims to 'respect the local legal order' (Section 10). 'For that reason', the Charter continues – that is, out of a contractual obligation, not from a belief in the intrinsic merit of liberal democracy – 'Muslims affirm the liberal–democratic order of the Federal Republic of Germany, including party pluralism, women's right to vote, and religious liberty' (Section 11). And, again, 'for that reason' (namely contractual obligation), Muslims 'accept the right to change one's religion, to have another religion or no religion at all' (ibid.). When asked whether he considered the principles of the secular state as an 'unalterable basis' for Muslims, the president of CCMG, Nadeem Elyas, responded evasively: 'Yes – as long as Muslims are in the minority' (Ammann 2004: 86). This was consistent because, once Muslims constituted the majority, the 'contract' was void and another set of laws, that of the 'House of Islam', applied.

Of course, whether liberal democracy is embraced instrumentally or intrinsically is irrelevant from a liberal point of view, which in the liberal state is also the legal point of view. As the German Constitutional Court held in its decision on Jehova's Witnesses, all that the liberal state can expect from its members is external conformity with the law; it would violate the principle of liberal neutrality to prescribe peoples' inner convictions. The often raised question whether Islam is compatible with liberal democracy is thus 'not legitimate' (Bielefeld 2006: 153) – not to mention that the absence of an 'institutionalized authority with binding interpretive competence' in Islam makes it impossible to say what 'Islam' actually is.[10] And, as Peter Sahlins (1989) has demonstrated in an altogether different context, instrumentally adopted identifications may eventually grow into intrinsically held identities.

Still, the distance between Islamic doctrine and the integration policies of European states, whose professed goal, to quote one example, is to transform 'Muslims in Germany' into 'German Muslims', is considerable.[11] This also seems to be the main reason why multiculturalism has been in retreat throughout western Europe in the past decade or so (see Joppke 2004). Reflecting on the recent difficulties of 'liberal multiculturalism', Will Kymlicka (2007: 4–6) identified two conditions required in order for it to work: first, there has to be a 'desecuritization' of the state–minority relations, so that a minority is not perceived as a 'fifth column' which undermines the geo-political integrity of the state; secondly, there has to be a 'liberal–democratic consensus' on the part of the minority which assures the majority that, if granted minority rights, this minority will not erect 'islands of local tyranny' within the broader state. The absence of both conditions, Kymlicka concludes, 'help[s] explain the partial retreat from multiculturalism in some countries in relation to recent Muslim immigrants, who are often seen as both disloyal and illiberal' (p. 6).

The presumed disloyalty and illiberalism of Muslim immigrants is the main backdrop to the rise of 'civic integration' policies in Europe. Next to language learning, these policies require newcomers to familiarize themselves with the general principles and institutions of liberal democracy and with their particular incarnation in the respective host country (for an overview, see Joppke 2007b). These policies have a 'neo-liberal' market component, growing stronger under contemporary globalization, according to which newcomers are to become 'self-sufficient' instead of being a costly burden on the welfare state.[12] But civic integration also has a liberal identity component, which cannot be decoupled from the fact that the target population of civic integration is mostly Muslim. Earlier I interpreted civic integration as an instance of 'repressive liberalism' (ibid.), in the relatively trivial sense that liberal goals are pursued with illiberal means (especially *obliging* newcomers to take language and civics classes). But an obligation is not *ipso facto* repressive. Instead, one has to consider, further, whether the policy merely expects newcomers to be cognizant of liberal–democratic norms and to observe them in their external behavior, which is an entirely legitimate expectation; *or* whether there is a deeper, more questionable ambition that newcomers should identify with these norms inwardly, plus a deployment of the state's mighty police powers to establish and control these identities. The notion of 'repressive liberalism' should be reserved to the latter program. While the distinction between external behavior and internal conviction may be difficult to draw in the real world, it is crucially important at an analytical level. Much as the liberal state might wish its members to identify with liberal norms (which cannot but be the goal of civic integration), it cannot legally force its members to do so. If it did, it would cease to be a liberal state.

To the degree that civic integration limits itself to a cognitive function and abstains from forcing identities on people, as it predominantly does, it should not be called 'repressive'. And where the line between the two is crossed, the policy immediately raises eyebrows and stands to be corrected. A notorious example is the so-called *Gesprächsleitfaden* ('interview guideline') issued by the regional government of Baden-Württemberg in early 2006, to help its naturalization officers to determine whether the formal 'acceptance' of the liberal–democratic order from applicants for citizenship corresponded to their 'real convictions'. The test was especially criticized because it targeted only Muslim applicants for citizenship and thus was blatantly discriminatory; in consequence, it was quickly withdrawn (see Joppke 2007b: 15). However, an equally questionable aspect of it was a thick understanding of liberal–democratic norms as something that one had not just to observe externally but to agree with internally. In this respect it was rightly denounced as a 'morality test' (*Gesinnungstest*). The idea behind it is that the liberal state would be a state for a distinct kind of people, namely liberal people – which, of course, is a profoundly illiberal idea.

Also, if it observes the distinction between following a norm and identifying with it, civic integration cannot be called a return to older programs of assimilation, like the 'Americanization' campaign of the early twentieth century. It remains instead within the ambit of 'integration'. The difference between the two is that assimilation is transitive, whereas integration is intransitive (see Brubaker 2003: 51; Albers 1994: 989). In the former, immigrants are objects; in the latter they are subjects. Assimilation is done by others; integration is done by oneself – it is self-integration. In this respect, policy can only provide incentives for choice, but choice itself has to be left to the individual. The outcome may well be, perhaps even should be, 'assimilation', if this is understood as the 'unintended consequence of myriad individual actions and choices in particular, social, cultural, economic, and political contexts' (Brubaker 2003: 52).

In light of these remarks, one might argue that civic integration is not as innocent as suggested above, because an obligation is the opposite of choice, and 'choice' is what distinguishes 'integration' from 'assimilation'. However, what civic integration brings to the fore is that we are dealing with immigrants. Their admittance is in principle discretionary, and they thus necessarily hold a lesser status than ordinary citizens. Indeed, the novelty of civic integration is to tie integration with migration control functions, which so far had been kept strictly separate (Joppke 2007b: 7–8). But the separation between the two, which in retrospect must be considered the happy moment when we were 'all multiculturalists' (Glazer 1997), was itself based on forgetting that one dealt with 'immigrants' as persons with lesser rights, at least as long as one acknowledges the right of states to have an immigration policy.

Having cleared civic integration of some of the charges often brought against it, one must realize that Muslim integration raises anew the old problem of the toleration of the intolerant. This is perhaps *the* problem of liberalism, and one that cannot be consistently resolved within its ambit. In Thomas Scanlon's useful definition, 'tolerance requires us to accept people and permit their practices even when we strongly disapprove of them'. This makes it a 'puzzling' attitude, an intermediate between 'wholehearted acceptance' and 'unrestrained opposition' (Scanlon 2003: 187). Furthermore, Scanlon calls it a 'risky policy with high stakes', not so much on account of the threat to formal laws and institutions which the intolerant represent as for their informal powers 'constantly' to 'redefine' the 'nature of society' (p. 201). For John Rawls, toleration of the intolerant should go very far, for the sake of 'equal citizenship',[13] but it should stop where a society's 'security' and 'institutions of liberty' are put in danger (Rawls 1971: 220). Headscarf laws and restrictions may be understood as navigating the limits of toleration.

By the same token, one realizes the overbearing ambition of 'multicultural recognition' (see e.g. Parekh 2000), which goes beyond mere 'toleration' and asks for 'wholehearted acceptance' of behavior that is generally disapproved of. For Tariq Ramadan, Europe's leading Muslim intellectual, Muslims expect 'more than a simple discourse of integration' (which is, presumably, liberal toleration); 'real integration' for them would require 'respect and mutual knowledge', which is more akin to Scanlon's 'wholehearted acceptance' (Ramadan, quoted in Joppke 2007a: 339). But how could one expect a secular feminist to 'accept wholeheartedly' the Islamic veil, which, irrespective of its innumerable variations and possible modernity, cannot but signify submission – to God, to men, or to both? All that can be reasonably expected is a toleration of the veil, because – short of being forcibly re-educated (which is what multiculturalism may boil down to, with respect to the majority) – how can one approve of something that one disapproves of? But there are limits to toleration, and they inevitably vary according to time, place, and circumstance.

Confusingly, both France's wholesale attack on the Islamic headscarf and Britain's hands-off attitude towards it fall within the ambit of liberalism. Liberalism is, at heart, 'a project of toleration that began in Europe in the sixteenth century' (Gray 2000: 1). But, as John Gray elaborates further, it is a project with two faces. In the older, Hobbesian variant, liberalism is an institutional modus vivendi which allows many diverse ways of life to co-exist peacefully, without the presumption of overarching common values. In the other, Enlightenment-inspired and Lockean version, liberalism is a more ambitious ethical project of finding a 'rational consensus on values' and of arriving at an 'ideal form of life' within a 'universal regime' (pp. 2–3). Gray's sympathy is with the Hobbesian version, which he takes to provide the only viable response to the contemporary challenge of 'deep diversity' (that consensus liberals like John Locke, who bickered about diversity *within* Protestant Christianity, could not even remotely be aware of).

However, it is more reasonable to assume that liberalism requires both *laisser-faire* and ethical consensus as its constituent elements and that, if not checked by a modicum of the other element, a one-sided liberalism is likely to destroy itself. I take this to be the message of the French and British headscarf controversies. Both countries represented, in crystalline form, the two faces of liberalism: modus vivendi in Britain and ethical consensus in France. Modus vivendi liberalism is conducive to extreme claims, such as by head-to-toe veiled teachers. And there is no built-in stopping point, because of an inevitably weak sense of the collective self. If Britain indeed is, as multiculturalists would like it, a 'community of communities' (Parekh 2001), all cathectic energy is spent at lower levels, so that the meta-community must forever remain in search of itself. Conversely, the ethical consensus liberalism of France, which stipulates abstract individuals devoid of all their origin features, becomes indistinguishable from a nationalism which threatens individual liberties and liberalism itself. Only Germany remained strangely outside the duopoly of liberalism, and liberalism appeared here in the extraneous form of arcane court legalese. The one plain language that surfaced in Germany's headscarf controversy was that of a nationalism untouched by universalistic impulse, which says that 'we' happen to be one thing, 'Christian–occidental', and 'they' another, 'Muslim', and never shall the two meet.

Luckily there have been self-corrective forces at work, by means of which the ignored pole of liberalism (modus vivendi in France, rational consensus in Britain) or a denigrated liberalism as such (as in Germany) asserted itself. Accordingly, in France, laicity meant not just political republicanism but also religious liberties, which were mobilized by the legal system against headscarf exclusions. In Britain, where the political state largely stayed outside the fray, it was the legal system that corrected headscarf extremism, cautiously bringing to bear some collectivity oriented values, though in the understated form of protecting third-party rights or ensuring efficient classroom communication. In Germany, the jurisdiction of the Constitutional Court stands for liberalism *sans phrase*, in its insistence that restrictiveness of religious wear would have to apply to all religions equally and not just to Islam. It cannot but clash with the regional governments' crusade against Islam under the Christian–occidental banner, yet the outcome of this clash is still undetermined.

It was the central claim of this book that the Islamic headscarf functioned as a mirror of identity. What are the identities reflected in it? The answer is: more than one in any one country, and increasingly less national ones. Rogers Brubaker and Frederick Cooper (2000) rightly pointed out that the concept of identity is one of the most overused yet underspecified concepts in the social sciences. I gave in to using it only reluctantly, for lack of a better word. But the mechanism addressed in these terms is unavoidable and of disarming simplicity: 'Descriptions of the other [. . .] always imply self-descriptions' (Amir-Moazami 2007: 17). This does not imply that descriptions of the self have to be made by way of negating or excluding otherness. A young Canadian political theorist (Abizadeh 2005) argued convincingly that collective identities cannot be modeled on individual identities; they may spring from an internal dialogue that needs no excluded other. All civic identities, from French republicanism to German constitutional patriotism, work this way: they are generated in time more than in space, by a collectivity's dialogue with its own past rather than through demarcation from another collectivity. 'Europe', whose leaders refused to include a reference to Christianity into its proposed constitution and whose official criteria for admissions do not know any geographic or ethnocultural limitation,[14] works much the same way. It requires a lot of negative energy to see in it a 'closed Christian club'.

It is true, headscarf laws reflect a new emphasis in European states on nationalizing their immigrant populations, and in this they complement the new policies of civic integration. However, if one insists on calling this 'nation-building', it is a rather light version of it.[15] Nations, which had once inherited from their religious predecessors the aura of the sacred, have inevitably lost it – at least in the western heartland of unifying Europe. Citizenship and nationhood once implied a 'transcendence' from one's primordial origins. As Dominique Schnapper (2006) claims for the most 'transcendent' nation of all, even in France there has been a withering of this notion, because the contemporary interventionist state makes the 'political community coincide with the real, concrete society' (p. 192). The rise of diversity, which is now the master rhetoric in all western states, France included, signifies the decline of political transcendence. The chronic individualization and diversification of lifestyles, in combination with the omnivorous state interventionism of late modernity, fatally weakens the private–public distinction, on which the transcendence of the nation once rested. This is the one structural opening for Muslims that will outlast all headscarf laws and civic integration policies. It may be phrased in terms of the question: 'Why should Muslims shut up if Gays speak out?' (Tietze 2001: 197).

In the twenty-first century, the internal diversity of society is considered legitimate and cannot be smashed. Thus it is no surprise that states find it ever more difficult to instil national particularism through their immigrant and ethnic minority integration policies. And the national self-definitions that inevitably frame such policies fall out along essentially identical lines, as repetitions of the self-same creed of liberal democracy (see Joppke 2008). The social logic of this has been crisply articulated by Georg Simmel (1971: 257): '[T]he elements of a distinctive social circle are undifferentiated, and the elements of a circle that is not distinctive are differentiated.' With the help of this formula one can easily see why twenty-first-century nation-building cannot be a replica of nineteenth-century nation-building. The sharply developed particularisms of nineteenth-century nations rested on the enforced sameness of the individuals and groups that constituted them, the military uniform being the foremost symbol of the sameness of the parts and distinctness of the whole which marked the classic nation–state. By contrast, twenty-first-century nation-building occurs in the context of highly pluralistic and individualized societies, where individual and group particularism is protected under the flag of 'diversity'. In such a setting, collective self-descriptions must be ever more general and abstract, to the point of becoming exchangeable, in order to encompass this diversity. This is why contemporary definitions of what it means to be French, British, German, and so forth are all so similar.

This is good news for Muslims, as for all minorities, because narrowly ethnic and religious self-definitions are inevitably losing ground in pluralistic and differentiated societies, in favor of political self-definitions *à l'américaine* or *à la française*. As France and Britain are within the continuum of liberalism, which is the classic formula of accommodating diversity since Hobbes' days, Muslims are in different ways included in both: in terms of an understated modus vivendi in Britain, but also in terms of an ethically more ambitious consensus in France. I thus take issue, again, with Joan Scott's assertion that the French headscarf ban showed that 'one could not be both Muslim and French' and that 'assimilation was the only route to membership in the nation' (2007: 135). First, the concept of 'assimilation' has long been dropped in French political discourse, if perhaps a touch later than elsewhere, in favor of the concept of 'integration', which leaves the ethical integrity of the individual intact (see Joppke 2007b: 2). But, more importantly, to be French is not defined ethnically or religiously but politically, in terms of republicanism – France is America's 'sister republic' (Higonnet 1988). So there cannot be a competition between 'Muslim' (which is either ethnic or religious or both) and 'French' (which is always political). Both terms are simply located at different levels of abstraction and allegiance. Only if one defines 'Muslim' expansively, in political terms, can there be a competition of it with 'French'. But that would turn the tables on the Muslims: if to be 'Muslim' is to be member of a 'global Muslim nation' (Shavit 2007: 2), as Islamic doctrine indeed claims, then a person, qua Muslim, cannot be French (or British or German and so on). Then the problem is not with France, which excludes, but with Islam, which is incompatible with liberalism, most notably with its private–public distinction.

In this heavily mined terrain, one must distinguish carefully between what Islamic doctrine holds and what ordinary Muslims think or believe. With respect to the latter, the claimed impossibility to 'be both Muslim and French' (Scott 2007: 135) is implausible. French Muslims have mostly adopted the idiom of *laïcité*, the cornerstone of French republicanism, rather than staying aloof. A recent survey has found 78 percent of French Muslims being in support of *laïcité* (see Perry 2006: 21). This is because this concept is elastic, leaving space for nationalist *and* rights-oriented stances; and French Muslims have learned, to great effect until 2004, to mobilize the latter against the former. It is true, the headscarf law expresses a certain idea of France, but there are other ways of being French that can be only momentarily suppressed – including one that revolves around liberal laicity. Despite the victory of republican laicity in 2004, liberal laicity has not thereby disappeared.

The contrast with Germany is instructive in this respect. This is a case where Muslims are *really* excluded from a certain 'Christian–occidental' self-definition of the state, simply because one cannot be Christian and Muslim at the same time. This is the identity that transpires in the headscarf laws of the Catholic–conservative *Länder*. However, this is a legally contestable identity, which squarely contradicts the jurisdiction of Germany's highest court, the *Bundesverfassungsgericht*, from its 1995 Kruzifix decision to its 2003 Ludin decision, which has triggered the regional headscarf laws. And at federal level no one has ever dared to define the German state as a Christian state. There is one brief reference to 'God' in the preamble to the Basic Law, but only with respect to the special 'responsibility' of Germans to 'further world peace' after 1945. And this 'God' is not limited to the one of Christianity. Accordingly, it was not the federal government but the Catholic–conservative regional governments of Bavaria and Baden-Württemberg that pushed for a reference to the Christian God in the EU constitution, and without success. At federal level, the identity and demeanor of the German state after World War II has been thoroughly post-national, which is well-captured in Habermas' notion of 'constitutional patriotism'. *This* identity could never be legally tested in the German headscarf controversy, simply because the latter never involved the federal government but only the regional governments. However, should the Constitutional Court retain its previous stance of religious equality in the still evolving German headscarf story, *this* is the identity that cannot but prevail over the regions' resurrection of an ethnic nationalism that does not dare to speak its name.

Finally, is there a 'best practice' in dealing with the Islamic headscarf in western Europe, which could even serve as a model for all liberal states? Having recently spilled over from the business lexicon to the political lexicon (especially in the jargon-plagued European Union), the notion of 'best practice' depicts a world which is flat, without history and institutional idiosyncrasy – a world like McDonald's (though that is surely worst practice in its own domain). There has been much reflection lately on best religious 'governance' (Bader 2007), as if the slate of historically established state-church regimes could ever be wiped clean. Certainly, with respect to the Islamic headscarf one cannot but admire the British solution of keeping the conflict local and of neutralizing its political dimension by reducing the matter to one of effective communication as a benchmark for intervention. But the fact that Britain is now routinely forced to deal with rather extremist claims, at considerable public expense, suggests that this cannot be the best of all religious governance worlds. Moreover, British Muslims, though pampered by a uniquely accommodating government, rank among the most dissatisfied and alienated Muslim minorities of Europe, which casts a long shadow over Britain's liberal multiculturalism (Joppke 2009).

By contrast, France has seen nothing of this. This is despite the fact that this country is usually attacked for its heavy line on the headscarf, deemed only to alienate her Muslims and to fuel further Islamic extremism. When asked in a Pew Research Center survey in 2006 whether there is a 'conflict between being a devout Muslim and living in a modern society', only 28 percent of French Muslims thought there was a conflict – but 47 percent of British Muslims thought so (Pew Research Center 2006: 3). Similarly, French Muslims are notably less likely than British Muslims to view 'people in western countries' as 'selfish' (51 versus 67 percent), 'arrogant' (45 versus 64 percent), 'violent' (29 versus 52 percent), 'greedy' (31 versus 63 percent), 'immoral' (30 versus 57 percent), and 'fanatical' (26 versus 44 percent) (p. 13). And an impressive 91 percent of French Muslims expressed 'favorable opinions of Christians', whereas only (but still) 71 percent of British Muslims did so (ibid. 11). Conversely, however, non-Muslim majorities in both countries hold similarly positive views on Muslim minorities (ibid. 16). One must conclude that French Muslims are culturally much better integrated than British Muslims. Have French Muslims not noticed that they are considered 'lesser people' by the French majority (as argued by Scott 2007: 45)?

In reality, France is the only country in Europe to confront its Muslim minority with an attitude, and one that has paid off. This is because it has not been an attitude of exclusion or racism, as some have argued, but of setting clear and equal terms of integration. Muslims have understood and accepted these terms. One forgets that Bretons (and innumerable other regional minorities) had to give up their *patois* to become French. No such sacrifice is expected of Muslims – they can practise their religion, as they should in a liberal state, on terms that nominally are the same for *all* religions, native Catholicism included. Factual disadvantage that results from not having been there first is increasingly tackled by a pro-active state. Under President Sarkozy, not even laicity is any longer sacrosanct. His vision of a 'positive laicity', in which religion is perceived not as a 'threat' but as an 'asset' to the state, was strategically offered to audiences in Rome and Riyad alike.[16] In a punchy discussion of how Europe might master the twenty-first-century migrations, Randall Hansen (2007: 16) prescribed the dual medicine of 'free economy and Jacobin state': 'If Europe is to cope with a new century of immigration, it needs labour market policies *à l'américaine* and integration policies *à la française.*' He may exaggerate the stability of French republicanism – the headscarf law might well be registered as its swan-song by future historians. But what France has more than other European countries is a 'clear integration framework reflecting values they [*sc.* the receiving countries] confidently hold' (p. 16).

If one disregards the inevitable downsides of their respective liberalisms, the British and the French extreme in dealing with the Islamic headscarf both seem to work in their own terms. 'Best practice' talk is pointless here. However, undoubtedly the 'worst practice' in western Europe's dealings with the headscarf is the German stance of saying 'no' to Islam but 'yes' to Christianity. More than telling its Muslims that they can never be 'in', this gives a silently racist majority the license to call them 'out'. The recent Pew Research Center survey (2006: 3) accordingly found that the German Muslims' views of their host society were generally moderate to positive; as was argued earlier, they are not sufficiently a part of German society to think anything else. What stood out were the majority's staunchly negative views of the Muslim minority: 70 percent of the Germans surveyed believe that there is a 'conflict between being a devout Muslim and living in a modern society' (p. 3), and 78 percent even hold Muslims to be 'fanatical' (p. 5). It would be off the mark to claim that there is a causal connection between such views and the selective restrictions on the headscarf from some (in fact from most) regional governments. But the message that ordinary Germans hear from some of their elected leaders is that our society is 'Christian–occidental' and that thus we may be partial – for Christianity and against Islam. In this view, notably the German (not the French) Muslims are 'lesser people' indeed, at least with respect to the treatment the state owes them. This is the position that stands to be corrected if liberalism is to prevail.

Notes

Chapter 1   The Islamic Headscarf in Western Europe

1   This book uses the words 'headscarf' and 'veil' interchangeably (unless further specified), to denote a species of face wear, head wear, or body wear for women that is prescribed by Islam to hide their bodily contours. The general Arabic word for this is *hijab*, which means 'cover' or 'curtain'. But there are multiple styles of such wear; they vary according to region, tradition, and era and are designated by different Arabic words (such as *jilbab*, *niqab*, or *burka*, to mention only some of the more extreme types). See El Guindi (2001).

2   Originating in Arabic countries, the *jilbab* is 'an unfitted, long-sleeved, ankle-length gown in austere solid colours and thick opaque fabric' (*Oxford Encyclopedia of the Modern Islamic World*, quoted in Shadid and Koningsveld 2005: 35). The *jilbab* is often combined with a *niqab*, which is a face veil that leaves only two eye-slits.

3   Department of Justice, 'Justice Department Reaches Settlement Agreement with Oklahoma School District in Muslim Student Headscarf Case' (19 May 2004), http://www.usdoj.gov/opa/pr/2004/May/04_crt_343.htm (last accessed 3 June 2008).

4   But see the interesting interpretation of Chirac's statement by Joan Scott (2007: 159), for whom 'the aggression of the woman consisted in denying (French) men the pleasure – understood as a natural right [. . .] – to see behind the veil. This was taken to be an assault on male sexuality, a kind of castration.' Scott further argues that the French obsession with the headscarf springs from a 'clash of gender systems' (p. 168), the Islamic one 'recognizing' and the French 'denying' the threat of female sexuality to their respective ideological frames (Islam

and republicanism). This is a weirdly brilliant exculpation of the subjugation of women in Islam.

5   Surah 24(30), reproduced in the *Koran* (2003: 248).

6   This term has been suggested by my research assistant, Leyla Arslan.

7   For a French–German comparison in the spirit of Mahmood (2005), see Jouili and Amir-Moazami (2006).

8   Decision of the German Federal Constitutional Court, BVerfGE 102, 370 (Körperschaftsstatus der Zeugen Jehovas), p. 17.

9   On Britain as a 'stateless' society, see also the classic account by Dyson (1980) and, more recently, Laborde (2000).

10 Agence France Press, 16 October 2006 (from Lexis–Nexis).

11 Department for Education and Skills (DfES), *Guidance to Schools on School Uniform Related Policies* (London, 20 March 2007), p. 7.

12 Shadow Home Minister David Davis, 'Do Muslims really want apartheid here?', *Sunday Telegraph*, 15 October 2006, p. 24.

13 *International Herald Tribune*, 23 October 2006, p. 3.

14 *Guardian*, 6 October 2006.

15 *Daily Mail*, 11 October 2006, p. 15.

16 This is Timothy Garton Ash's contemptuous verdict on Hirsi Ali, in his review essay 'Islam in Europe', *New York Review of Books* 53(15), 5 October 2006.

17 From Hirsi Ali's book *The Caged Virgin*, quoted in the *Independent* of 8 July 2006, p. 11.

Chapter 2   The Pupil's Headscarf in Republican France

1   In 2003, that is, before the headscarf ban, there were only 1,254 counted *hijab* wearers among France's 250,000 Muslim schoolgirls (Laurence and Vaisse 2006: 80).

2   The same could not be said with respect to socio-economic integration: the unemployment rate of French citizens of Algerian and Moroccan descent is currently at 30 percent, three times higher than that of the native French (Giry 2006: 5). In the infamous *cités*, the unemployment rate of Muslims is over 40 percent (Laurence and Vaisse 2006: 38).

3   Then Minister of the Interior Nicolas Sarkozy has referred to his push for a representative French Muslim organization in terms of 'inviting Islam to the dining-table of the republic' (e.g. in *Le Figaro*, 12 September 2003).

4   *Le Monde*, 14 November 2007, p. 9.

5   According to the 1905 Law on the Separation of Church and State, the state owns all the churches built before 1905. In reality, this meant maintenance of the pre-1905 church buildings at the state's expense. In addition, the state organizes and finances offices of chaplain in closed institutions (prisons, schools, hospitals) and at airports; provides for religious representation on public television; and pays the salaries of teachers at state-supported religious schools (see Bowen 2007a: 1010).

6   *Le Figaro*, 21 April 2003.

7   The word *laïque* first appeared in Article 1 of the 1946 Constitution: 'France is an indivisible, *laïque*, democratic, and social republic.'

8   The distinction between a 'liberal' and a 'republican' form of laicity, used here and in the following sections, should not let us forget that republicanism is itself a variant of privatizing religion, that is, of liberalism, as discussed earlier; however, it is a variant that may take on illiberal features, as the course of the headscarf controversy itself attests.

9   *Le Figaro*, 12 September 2003.

10   E. Badinter, R. Debray, A. Finkielkraut, E. de Fontenay and C. Kintzler, 'Profs, ne capitulons pas!', *Le Nouvel Observateur*, 2 November 1989.

11   Ibid.

12   Ibid.

13   Arrêt du Conseil d'Etat, 2 November 1992, M. Kherouaa et Mme. Kachour, M. Balo et Mme. Kizic (reprinted in *Revue française de droit administratif*, 9/1, 1993, 118f).

14   Avis du Conseil d'Etat, 27 November 1989, reprinted in William (1991; emphasis mine).

15   From 'Profs, ne capitulons pas!', quoted above.

16   Circulaire no 1649 of 20 September 1994 (Education nationale, Jeunesse et Sports: 'Neutralité de l'enseignement public: Port de signes ostentatoires dans les établissements scolaires').

17   Thomas Milcent ('Dr Abdallah'), in his testimony to the Debré Commission (Debré Rapport 2003: tome II, 2ème partie, p. 36).

18   Circulaire du 12 décembre 1989 (Education nationale, Jeunesse et Sports : 'Laïcité, port de signes religieux par les élèves et caractère obligatoire des enseignements').

19   Circulaire no 1649 du 20 septémbre 1994 (see above).

20   In fact, this 'republican law' was not cast in stone. A March 1991 *circulaire* had allowed 'women belonging to a religious order' to be photographed with a veil; originally meant for Catholic nuns,

this exemption was extended to Muslims, 'on the condition that their face was completely uncovered and perfectly identifiable'. Only a November 1994 *circulaire* prescribed that photographs should be taken *tête nue*. Overall, there was a constant to and fro around this 'republican' requirement over the past two decades (see Gresh 2004: 277).

21 As Bowen (2006: 123) notes, between September 2003 and February 2004 there was an average of two articles per day on the Islamic headscarf in each of the three major French newspapers (*Le Monde, Le Figaro, La Libération*).

22 A good account may be found in *Le Figaro*, 3 February 2004.

23 Xavier Ternisien, 'Pourquoi la polémique sur le foulard à l'école?', *Le Monde*, 17 June 2003.

24 For a more realistic picture stating the 'withering of political Islamism' and the 'depoliticization of young Muslims' in France, see International Crisis Group (2006).

25 G. Bapt (PS), *Assemblée Nationale*, 3 February 2004, 2ème séance, p. 1337.

26 'Discours prononcé par Jacques Chirac, Président de la République Française, relatif au respect du principe de laïcité dans la République', 17 December 2003, Elysée Palace, Paris (accessed through http://www.aidh.org/laic/pres-17-12-chirac.htm).

27 Prime Minister Raffarin addressing the *Assemblée Nationale*, 3 February 2004, 2e séance.

28 Quoted from the *Assemblée Nationale*, 148ème séance and 149ème séance, 3 February 2004.

29 M. Long and P. Weil, 'La laïcité en voie d'adaptation', *La Libération*, 26 January 2004, p. 39.

30 Bernard Accoyer (UMP), *Assemblée Nationale*, 3 February 2004, 3ème séance.

31 From Sarkozy's testimony before the Debré Commission (Debré Rapport 2003: tome 3, 6ème partie, pp. 119, 115, and 118 respectively).

32 The word used by the then Minister of Education François Fillon (*Le Figaro*, 9 September 2004).

Chapter 3   The Teacher's Headscarf in Christian–
Occidental Germany

1 Of course, the distinction between 'religious' and 'political' is modelled on a certain (Christian, or more precisely Protestant)

understanding of religion that cannot be generalized to all of them, and especially not to Islam (see Chapters 1 and 5). The distinction also rules out, by conceptual fiat, the possibility that the incriminated features of Islam, for instance the subordination of women, may be connected to Islam's religious core. While meant as a weapon against (certain variants of) Islam, the 'religious' versus 'political' distinction is at the same time strangely exculpating Islam.

2   Quoted in Oestreich (2004: 38). This opening salvo expressed the refusal of the Minister of the Interior Schavan, in July 1998, to employ aspiring teacher Fereshta Ludin.

3   For an impressionistic overview, see 'Haben wir schon die Scharia,' *Der Spiegel* 26 March 2007, pp. 22ff. This overview was triggered by the scandalous refusal by a local (female!) judge in Frankfurt to expedite the divorce request of a German–Moroccan woman who, in the opinion of this judge, had to 'count on' being beaten up by her Muslim husband because of his religious 'right to beat' his wife (*Züchtigungsrecht*) according to Sure 4, verse 34 of the Koran (cited in Court!).

4   Decision of the Federal Administrative Court (6th Senate), 25 August 1993 (6 C 8/91).

5   Ibid.

6   Decision of the Upper Administrative Court of North Rhine-Westphalia (19th Senate), 17 January 2002 (19 B 99/02).

7   This was the formula decreed in the 1993 FAC landmark rule (see above).

8   For a description of the situation in Frankfurt's public schools, see 'Das Übliche', *Frankfurter Allgemeine Zeitung*, 22 December 2004, p. 3.

9   Decision of the Federal Constitutional Court on the 'Simultanschule', 17 December 1975 (BVerfGE 41, 29).

10 Decision of the Federal Constitutional Court on the 'Kruzifix', 16 May 1995 (1 BvR 1087/91).

11 For this distinction, see Chapter 4.

12 Decision of the Federal Constitutional Court on 'Jehovah's Witnesses', 19 December 2000 (BVerfGE 102, 370).

13 Ibid.

14 *Stand der rechtlichen Gleichstellung des Islam in Deutschland* (German Parliament: BT-Drucksache Nr. 16/2085, 29 June 2006), p. 48.

15 This federal government response downplays the high (and apparently growing) degree of religiousness among German

Muslims, who are predominantly Turkish. A recent survey found 85 percent of German Turks responding that they were 'rather' or 'strictly' religious (*Economist*, 24 June 2006, p. 30). The 'enormously high importance of religion and religiousness for Muslims in Germany' is confirmed by a recent study commissioned by the Federal Ministry of the Interior, which found about 40 percent of the surveyed Muslims subscribing to 'fundamental orientations' (a euphemism for fundamentalism) (Brettfeld and Wetzels 2007: 492f).

16   Necla Kelek in *Süddeutsche Zeitung*, 23 April 2007, p. 2.

17   A religious Muslim leader objected to the participation of feminist Muslim critics at the first German Islam Conference in September 2006 in such terms: 'This is as if we tried to enter into a dialogue with Catholics, and for this purpose we invite the Pope and pop star Madonna' (*die tageszeitung* [TAZ], 29 September 2006). This misconstrues the purpose of the Islam Conference, which was never meant to be limited to religious groups, but aimed to establish a 'dialogue' with *all* German Muslims. However, the billing of the meeting in terms of 'Islam' (as opposed to 'Muslim') has contributed to this misunderstanding.

18   The quotation is from Minister of the Interior Wolfgang Schäuble (*Süddeutsche Zeitung*, 26 September 2006, p. 1). See also his opening speech at the first German Islam Conference, reprinted as 'Muslime in Deutschland' in *Frankfurter Allgemeine Zeitung*, 27 September 2006.

19   'Most Muslims who attend mosques happen to be religious-conservative', said Mounir Azzaoui, leader of a Muslim faction in the Green Party (*die tageszeitung* [TAZ], 20 April 2007, p. 12).

20   Werner Schiffauer, 'Die Türken, ein deutscher Glücksfall', *Frankfurter Allgemeine Sonntagszeitung*, 28 November 2004.

21   Ibid.

22   But see the *Economist* ('Two amalgamated worlds', 5 April 2008), which quotes intelligence officials for the view that, most recently, 'the amount of Turkish language material preaching *jihad* over the internet has exploded'.

23   Kretschmann (Greens), First Reading of anti-headscarf law, *Landtag Baden-Württemberg*, 4 February 2004, p. 4390.

24   As Nikola Tietze (2001: 187) observes, a collective self-definition in terms of 'Christian–occidental' allows 'to bypass the idiom of nation and still to allow for the idea of unity'. See also constitu-

tional justice Christine Hohmann-Dennhard, who argued that the reference to 'Christian–occidental' values' is a surrogate for the notions of 'nation and national', which have been delegitimized by German history. See her speech 'Vom Staat und den Werten, auf die sein Recht baut' (*Frankfurter Rundschau*, 17 February 2006).

25 Thomas Nipperdey, quoted in Tietze (2001: 193).

26 Kleinmann (FDP/DVP), *Landtag Baden-Württemberg*, 4 February 2004, p. 4397.

27 Paul Kirchhof, 'Die postsäkulare Gesellschaft', *Frankfurter Allgemeine Zeitung*, 3 June 2004.

28 Uwe Volkmann, 'Risse in der Rechtsordnung', *Frankfurter Allgemeine Zeitung*, 11 March 2004.

29 The plaintiff's claim, as summarized in Decision of the Federal Constitutional Court on 'Ludin' (BVerfGE, 2 BvR 1436/02), 24 September 2003, p. 5.

30 Decision of the Federal Administrative Court (BverwG 2C24.01), 4 July 2002, p. 7.

31 Ibid., p. 10.

32 Ibid., p. 9.

33 Decision of the Federal Constitutional Court on 'Ludin' (BVerfGE, 2 BvR 1436/02), 24 September 2003, p. 15.

34 Ibid., p. 17.

35 See Chapter 3, n.1.

36 *Landtag von Baden-Württemberg*, 4. Wahlperiode, 62. Sitzung, 4 February 2004, p. 4387.

37 BVerfGE, 2 BvR 1436/02, 24 September 2003, p. 15.

38 Ibid., pp. 13f.

39 *die tageszeitung* (TAZ), 4 June 2003.

40 Dissenting opinion of the Justices Jentsch, Di Fabio und Mellinghoff (BVerfGE, 2BvR 1436/02), p. 18.

41 Ibid., para. 85.

42 Ibid., para. 79.

43 Ibid., para. 102.

44 Josef Isensee, 'Grundrechtseifer und Amtsvergessenheit', *Frankfurter Allgemeine Zeitung*, 8 June 2004.

45 The speech is reprinted in *Frankfurter Rundschau*, 23 January 2004.

46 Jewish symbols are included in the 'Christian–occidental' nexus.

47 *Landtag von Baden-Württemberg*, 13. Wahlperiode, Drucksache 13/2793, 14 January 2003.

48 Professor Ferdinand Kirchhof, in Ausschuss für Schule, Jugend und Sport (2004), p. 11.

49 Ibid.

50 Deputy Kleinmann (FDP/DVP), *Landtag von Baden-Württemberg*, 13. Wahlperiode, 67. Sitzung, 1 April 2004, p. 4704.

51 A. Schavan (CDU), *Landtag von Baden-Württemberg*, 62. Sitzung, 4 February 2004, p. 4387.

52 Deputy Mack (CDU), *Landtag von Baden-Württemberg*, 67. Sitzung, 1 April 2004, p. 4710.

53 Deputy Wintruff (SPD), *Landtag von Baden-Württemberg*, 62. Sitzung, 4 February 2004, p. 4395.

54 Professors Mahrenholz, Jestaedt, and Böckenförde, in Ausschuss für Jugend, Schule, und Sport (2004).

55 Ibid., p. 47.

56 F. Kirchhof, ibid., p. 82f.

57 BVerfGE 41, 29 ('Simultanschule'), decision of 17 December 1975; the quotation is from Article 16 of the 1953 Constitution of Baden-Württemberg.

58 Ibid.

59 Beschlussempfehlung und Bericht des Ausschusses für Schule, Jugend und Sport (Drucksache 13/3071), 30 March 2004, p. 3.

60 *Landtag von Baden-Württemberg*, plenary session of 1 April 2004, p. 4719.

61 Ibid.

62 Ibid., p. 4724.

63 Deputy Kretschmann (Greens), *Landtag von Baden-Württemberg*, plenary session of 4 February 2004, p. 4389.

64 D.Haselbach, 'Zurückhaltung wird nur den Fremden auferlegt', *Frankfurter Allgemeine Zeitung*, 25 August 2004.

65 Kretschmann (Greens) and Wieser (CDU), *Landtag von Baden-Württemberg*, plenary session of 4 February 2004, p. 4406.

66 Ernst-Wolfgang Böckenförde, 'Ver[w]irrung im Kopftuchstreit', *Süddeutsche Zeitung*, 16 January 2004.

67 Decision of the Federal Administrative Court (BverwG 2c45.03), 24 June 2004, p. 10.

68 Ibid., p. 13.

69 Interview with E.W.Böckenförde, *Süddeutsche Zeitung*, 13 October 2004, p. 6.

70 *Landtag von Baden-Württemberg*, 13. Wahlperiode, Drucksache 13/3679, 20 October 2004.

71 Martin Kriele, 'Wer glaubt's?' *Frankfurter Allgemeine Zeitung*, 17 February 2005.

72   Decision of the Federal Constitutional Court on the Crucifix, 16 May 1995 (1 BvR 1087/91).
73   Staatsgerichtshof of the Hesse Land, decision of 10 December 2007 (P.St. 2016); p. 33.
74   Ibid., p. 34.
75   Ibid., p. 60.
76   *Frankfurter Rundschau*, 11 December 2007.

Chapter 4   The Extreme Headscarf in Multicultural Britain

1   'A new brand for Britain', *Economist*, 23 August 1997, 25f.
2   *Daily Telegraph*, 27 December 2003, p. 4.
3   Mary Riddell, 'Veiled threats', *Observer*, 14 December 2003, p. 26.
4   *Lancashire Telegraph*, 5 October 2006 (reprinted in *Guardian*, 6 October 2006).
5   Retrieved from Hermes Database, 7 July 2004 (Lexis-Nexis).
6   Ibid. This is a present-oriented view which ignores the fact that, as an 'imperial people', the English/British historically had a 'missionary' sense of themselves (see Kumar 2006).
7   Ibid.
8   Democratic or ethical liberalism, of course, branches out into civic republicanism. For a brilliant discussion of the indeterminacy of each as a philosophy of public education, see Stolzenberg (1993).
9   A head teacher of a predominantly Muslim primary school in Birmingham, quoted in Fetzer and Soper (2005: 40).
10   *Daily Telegraph*, 2 September 2005, p. 7.
11   To be included in the antiquated (and largely dormant) Law on Blasphemy, which would allow them to ban literature and other artistic and public expressions deemed injurious to their religious sentiments, was the main demand of British Muslims after the publication of Salman Rushdie's *Satanic Verses* in 1989. This demand was resolutely rejected by the Thatcher government.
12   Note that the Queen has recently established a prayer room in Windsor Castle for the royal residence's *only* Muslim employee (*Express*, 30 September 2006, p. 13).
13   Poulter (1997: 64), citing the court case *Nyazi v. Rymans Ltd.* (1988).

14   *Guardian*, 12 June 1997, p. 9.

15   For instance, ECHR protection is only against public authorities, whereas discrimination law applies also to private individuals and bodies (see Blair 2005: 408f).

16   Quoted in the *Observer* of 29 December 1996, p. 12.

17   Figures in the Labour Force Survey 2005 show that only 23% of Pakistani and Bangladeshi women between 16 and 34 *want* to work; see Policy Exchange (2007: 69).

18   'From brick land to the fast lane', *Economist*, 27 October 2007, p. 46.

19   Home Office, 22 October 1997 (Hermes database, retrieved through Lexis-Nexis).

20   Melanie Phillips, 'This lethal moral madness', *Daily Mail* 14 July 2005, pp. 14–15.

21   *Independent*, 12 July 2005, p. 2.

22   *Daily Mail*, 14 July 2005, pp. 14–15.

23   *Sunday Express*, 10 July 2005, p. 23.

24   *Mirror*, 18 July 2005, p. 23.

25   *Guardian*, 4 August 2005, p. 6.

26   Munira Mirza in *Daily Mail*, 29 January 2007, p. 4.

27   This and the following quotations are from Queen's Bench Division, *R (Begum)* v. *Headteacher and Governors of Denbigh H.S.* [2004] EWHC 1389 (Admin), [2004] ELR 374, 15 June 2004.

28   The fact that the *shalwar kameeze* was worn also by Hindu and Sikh pupils provided an important argument that no extra privilege should be granted to Muslims in allowing the *jilbab* (ibid., at para. 4).

29   The *jilbab* is a neck-to-toe cloak made of thick dark fabric which hides a woman's bodily contours completely, with the exception of face and hands.

30   I follow the instructive observations by NYU lawyer Paul Cruickshank, 'Covered faces, open rebellion', *International Herald Tribune*, 24 October 2006.

31   'Deconstructing the veil', *Economist*, 14 October 2006.

32   Judge Bennett, in Queen's Bench Division, *R (Begum)* v. *Headteacher* (above, n27), para. 17.

33   Ibid., para. 4.

34   Court of Appeal, *R (on the application of SB)* v. *Governors of Denbigh High School* [2005] EWCA Civ 199, 2 March 2005, at para. 3.

35   Queen's Bench Division, *R (Begum) v Headteacher* (above, n.27), at para. 15. In addition to local Muslim authorities, the London

Central Mosque and the Islamic Cultural Centre deemed the *shalwar kameeze* sufficient. But, as usual, for every expertise there is a counter-expertise. Two local Imams who had okayed the school uniform when consulted by the school apparently changed their minds when they were approached by Shabina Begum's lawyers six months later. The Centre for Islamic Studies in Birmingham likewise argued that the 'whole body' had to be covered, so that the *shalwar kameeze* was not sufficient (ibid., para. 20).

36   Ibid., para. 4.
37   Court of Appeal, *R (on the application of SB)* v. *Governors of Denbigh H.S.* [2005] EWCA Civ 199, 2 March 2005.
38   *Sahin* v. *Turkey* (2004) ECHR 44774/98, ECt HR.
39   Court of Appeal (above, n37), at para. 73.
40   Ibid., headnote.
41   House of Lords, *R (SB)* v. *Governors of Denbigh High School* [2006] UKHL 15, 22 March 2006.
42   Lord Bingham in ibid., at para. 31.
43   Lord Hoffmann in ibid., at para. 50.
44   After the Court of Appeal rule of March 2005, a picketing of schools 'by groups of young men who did appear to be from the more extreme of Muslim traditions' had been reported (Lord Bingham in ibid., para. 18).
45   Baroness Hale in ibid., at para. 97.
46   Lord Hoffmann in ibid., at para. 64.
47   Lord Bingham in ibid., at para. 2.
48   Tony Blair, quoted in *Evening Standard*, 29 November 2006, p. 5.
49   Jack Straw's intervention is reprinted in *Guardian*, 6 October 2006.
50   Ibid.
51   Employment Tribunal (Leeds), *Azmi* v. *Kirklees Metropolitan Council* (Case No 1801450/06), 6 October 2006; quoted from headnote.
52   Ibid.
53   Ibid., Judgment–1, at para. 3. 15.
54   Ibid., at para. 3. 14.
55   Ibid., at para. 3. 13.
56   Employment Appeal Tribunal, *Azmi* v. *Kirklees Metropolitan Borough Council* [2007] IRLR 484, 30 March 2007.
57   Employment Tribunal (Leeds), *Azmi* v. *Kirklees Metropolitan Council* (above, n51), at para. 9. 5.

58   Ibid., at para. 17.

59   Ibid., at para. 20.

60   Employment Appeal Tribunal, *Azmi* v. *Kirklees Metropolitan Borough Council* (above, n56) at para. 37.

61   Ibid.

62   Queen's Bench Division, *R (on the application of X)* v. *Head-teachers of Y School and Another* [2007] EWHC 298 (Admin), 21 February 2007.

63   *UK Newsquest Regional Press*, 7 February 2007.

64   *Agence France Press*, 8 February 2007.

65   Queen's Bench Division, *R (on the application of X)* v. *Head-teachers of Y School* (above, n.62), at para. 64.

66   Ibid.

67   Ibid., at para. 136.

68   Shadow Home Secretary David Davis in *Sunday Telegraph*, 15 October 2006, p. 24.

69   Y.Alibhai-Brown, 'We don't yet live in an Islamic Republic, so I will say it – I find the veil offensive', *Independent*, 9 October 2006, p. 37.

70   David Aaronovitch, 'Please don't rub your faith in my face', *Guardian*, 17 June 2003, p. 7.

71   Interview with Yanna, 35, a *niqab* wearer in London (*Evening Standard*, 14 November 2006, p. 18).

72   Ibid.

73   *Independent*, 9 October 2006, p. 37.

74   Ibid.

75   Yasmin Alibhai- Brown, quoted in *International Herald Tribune*, 23 October 2006, p. 3.

76   Allison Pearson, 'Here's why the veil so offends me', *Daily Mail*, 11 October 2006, p. 15.

77   See the open letter 'Important advice to the Muslim community in light of the debate over the veil' (17 October 2006), signed by 27 British Muslim leaders (including the Deputy Secretary General of the Muslim Council of Britain). Copy on file with author.

78   *Express*, 16 October 2006, p. 1.

79   *Mail on Sunday*, 17 September 2006, p. 41.

80   *The Times* (online), 20 December 2006.

81   Department for Education and Skills, 'Guidance to schools on school uniform related policies' (consultation document, 20 March 2007). Copy on file with author.

82   *Observer*, 19 March 2006, p. 7.

Chapter 5   Liberalism and Muslim Integration

1 See, for instance, the *Economist*'s special report 'Islam, America and Europe' (24 June 2006, pp. 29–31).

2 Ruth O'Brian, in her introduction to Scott (2007: viii), attributes this view to 'moderate Muslim groups', but the remainder of her text leaves little doubt that the view is close to her own: 'It [*sc.* the French headscarf controversy] [. . .] reveals the prejudices that white Judeo-Christian Europeans harbor against a portion of their nation's denizens [. . .] from their former colonies' (p. ix).

3 At the Parisian Institut Catholique, the so-called 'Catho'.

4 *Economist*, 24 June 2006, p. 30.

5 Representative for many, UMP deputy Yves Bur, *Assemblée Nationale*, 3ème séance, 3 February 2004, p. 1313.

6 For a strong argument that there are no 'European' but only 'western' values, see Winkler (2007).

7 Organized Muslims have propagated this too, especially after 2001. For instance, the 'Islamic Charter' of the Central Council of Muslims in Germany, issued in February 2002 to profess the compatibility of Islam with 'German state and society', starts with the claim that 'Islam is the religion of peace' ('the', not 'a'!), specifying that '"Islam" means both peace and submission'. This is etymologically wrong: the Arabic word *islâm* means only submission to the will of God, there is no reference to 'peace' in it (see Ammann 2004: 84).

8 Ahmet Senyurt, 'Spalten statt versöhnen', *Frankfurter Allgemeine Sonntagszeitung*, 8 August 2004, p. 8.

9 Zentralrat der Muslime in Deutschland, *Islamische Charta* (http://www.zentralrat.de/3035.php; last accessed 1 February 2008).

10 See Horst Dreier, 'Verfassungsstaat im Kampf der Kulturen', *Frankfurter Allgemeine Zeitung*, 4 October 2007, p. 10.

11 Wolfgang Schäuble (Federal Minister of the Interior), 'Muslims in Germany', *Frankfurter Allgemeine Zeitung*, 27 September 2006, p. 9.

12 For the over-representation of immigrants in western European welfare systems, see Koopmans (2005) and Hansen (2007).

13 This raises the question whether immigrants, as non-citizens, should be tolerated to the same length as citizens are. While I will not further pursue this question here, it goes without saying that the limits of toleration addressed below should apply even more to immigrants than to fellow-citizens.

14   The Copenhagen Criteria, issued at the 1993 European Council Summit in Copenhagen, mention only a functioning democracy, market economy, human rights protections, and implementation of European Community law as criteria of membership in the European Union.

15   For the real thing, consult Eugene Weber's classic study of nation-building in the French Third Republic (1976).

16   *Le Monde*, 18 January 2007, p. 10.

Bibliography

Abizadeh, Arash. 2005. 'Does collective identity presuppose an other?'. *American Political Science Review*, 99 (1), 45–60.

Abu-Lughod, Lila. 2002. 'Do Muslim women really need saving?'. *American Anthropologist*, 104 (3), 783–90.

Ahmed, Leyla. 1992. *Women and Gender in Islam*. New Haven: Yale University Press.

Albers, Hartmut. 1994. 'Glaubensfreiheit und schulische Integration von Ausländerkindern'. *Deutsches Verwaltungsblatt*, 1 September, 984–90.

Altinordu, Ates. 2004. *The Meaning(s) of the Headscarf*. Typescript.

Amara, Fadela. 2003. *Ni putes, ni soumises*. Paris: La Découverte.

Amir-Moazami, Schirin. 2004. *Discourses and Counter-Discourses: The Islamic Headscarf in the French and German Public Spheres*. Doctoral dissertation, European University Institute.

Amir-Moazami, Schirin. 2007. *Politisierte Religion*. Bielefeld: Transcript Verlag.

Ammann, Ludwig. 2004. *Cola und Koran*. Freiburg im Breisgau: Herder.

Ausschuss für Jugend, Schule, und Sport. 2004. *Gemeinsame öffentliche Anhörung des Ausschusses für Schule, Jugend und Sport und des Ständigen Ausschusses zu den Gesetzentwürfen zur Änderung des Schulgesetzes*. Stuttgart: 13. Landtag von Baden-Württemberg, 26. Sitzung des Ausschusses für Schule, Jugend und Sport, 12 March.

Avenarius, Hermann. 2002. 'Value orientation in German schools'. *Education and the Law*, 14 (1–2), 83–90.

Babés, Leïla. 1997. *L'Islam positif*. Paris: Ed. L'Atelier.

Bader, Johann. 2006. 'Gleichbehandlung von Kopftuch und Nonnenhabit?'. *Neue Zeitschrift für Verwaltungsrecht*, n. 12, 1333–7.

Bader, Veit. 2007. *Secularism or Democracy?* Amsterdam: Amsterdam University Press.

Badie, Bertrand and Pierre Birnbaum. 1983. *The Sociology of the State.* Chicago: University of Chicago Press.

Barbier, Maurice. 1993. 'Esquisse d'une théorie de la laïcité'. *Le Débat*, vol. 77, 73–88.

Barker, Ernest. 1951. *The Ideas and Ideals of the British Empire.* Cambridge: Cambridge University Press.

Barlas, Asma. 2002. *'Believing Women' in Islam.* Austin: University of Texas Press.

Basdevant-Gaudemet, Brigitte. 2000. 'The legal status of Islam in France'. In Silvio Ferrari and Anthony Bradney (eds), *Islam and European Legal Systems.* Aldershot: Ashgate.

Baubérot, Jean. 1990. *Vers un nouveau pacte laïque?* Paris: Seuil.

Baubérot, Jean. 2004. *Laïcité, 1905–2005.* Paris: Seuil.

Baubérot, Jean. 2005. 'Les mutations actuelles de la laïcité en France après la Commission Stasi'. Available at: http://jeanbauberotlaicite.blogspirit.com/archive/2005/04/19/laicite_2005.html (last accessed 5 March 2006).

Bellah, Robert. 1970. *Beyond Belief.* Berkeley: University of California Press.

Bielefeldt, Heiner. 2006. 'Islam und Grundgesetz'. In Ulrike Davy and Albrecht Weber (eds), *Paradigmenwechsel in Einwanderungsfragen?* Baden-Baden: Nomos.

Birnbaum, Pierre. 2001. *The Idea of France.* New York: Hill and Wang.

Blair, Ann. 2005. '*R (SB)* v. *Headteacher and Governors of Denbigh High School* – Human rights and religious dress in schools'. *Child and Family Law Quarterly*, 17 (3), 399–413.

Blair, Ann and Will Aps. 2005. 'What not to wear and other stories'. *Education and the Law* 17 (1–2), 1–22.

Böckenförde, Ernst-Wolfgang. 1967. 'Die Entstehung des Staates als Vorgang der Säkularisation'. In E. W. Böckenförde, *Recht, Staat, Freiheit,* Frankfurt am Main: Suhrkamp, 1991.

Böckenförde, Ernst-Wolfgang. 1973. 'Vorläufige Bilanz im Streit um das Schulgebet'. *Die Öffentliche Verwaltung*, 27 (8), 253–7.

Böckenförde, Ernst-Wolfgang. 2001. ' "Kopftuchstreit" auf dem richtigen Weg?'. *Neue Juristische Wochenschrift*, n. 10, 723–8.

Bourdieu, Pierre and Jean-Claude Passeron. 1970. *Reproduction in Education, Society and Culture.* London: Sage.

Bourdieu, Pierre and Loic Wacquant. 1992. *An Invitation to Reflexive Sociology.* Chicago: University of Chicago Press.

Bowen, John R. 2006. *Why the French Don't Like Headscarves.* Princeton: Princeton University Press.

Bowen, John R. 2007a. 'A view from France on the internal complexity of national models'. *Journal of Ethnic and Migration Studies*, 33 (6), 1003–16.

Bowen, John R. 2007b. *Recognizing Islam in France after 9/11.* Typescript.

Brenner, Emmanuel (ed.). 2003. *Les Territoires perdues de la république.* Paris: Editions Mille et une nuits.

Brettfeld, Katrin and Peter Wetzels. 2007. *Muslime in Deutschland.* Berlin: Federal Ministry of the Interior.

Brubaker, Rogers. 2003. 'The return of assimilation?'. In Christian Joppke and Ewa Morawska (eds), *Toward Assimilation and Citizenship,* London: Palgrave Macmillan.

Brubaker, Rogers and Fred Cooper. 2000. 'Beyond identity'. *Theory and Society*, 29 (1), 1–47.

Bundesministerium des Innern. 2008. *Deutsche Islam Konferenz (DIK): Zwischen-Resümee der Arbeitsgruppen und des Gesprächskreises.* Berlin, 13 March 2008.

Buruma, Ian and Avishai Margalit. 2004. *Occidentalism.* New York: Penguin.

Campenhausen, Axel Freiherr von. 2004. 'The German headscarf debate'. *Brigham Young University Law Review*, 665–99.

Cantle Report. 2001. *Community Cohesion.* London: Government Printing Office.

Carney, Damian and Adele Sinclair. 2006. 'School uniform revisited'. *Education and the Law*, 18 (2–3), 131–48.

Colley, Linda. 1992. *Britons.* New Haven: Yale University Press.

Commission on British Muslims and Islamophobia. 1997. *Islamophobia: A Challenge for Us All.* London: The Runnymede Trust.

Commission on British Muslims and Islamophobia. 2004. *Islamophobia: Issues, Challenges and Action.* Stoke-on-Trent (UK): Trentham Books.

Coq, Guy. 2003. *Laïcité et république.* Paris: Editions du Félin.

Davies, Gareth. 2005. 'Banning the jilbab'. *European Constitutional Law Review*, 1, 511–30.

Debray, Régis. 1990. 'La Laïcité: Une exception française'. In Hubert Bost (ed.), *Genèse et enjeux de la laïcité*, Genève: Labor et Fides.

Debré Rapport. 2003. *Rapport fait au nom de la mission d'information sur la question du port des signes religieux à l'école.* Paris: Assemblée Nationale, no 1275.

Dyson, Kenneth. 1980. *The State Tradition in Western Europe.* Oxford: Oxford University Press.

El Guindi, Fadwa. 1981. 'Veiling Infitah with Muslim ethic'. *Social Problems*, 28 (4), 465–85.

El Guindi, Fadwa. 2001. 'Hijab'. In Oxford Encyclopedia of the Modern Islamic World (edited by John Esposito), vol.2. New York: Oxford University Press, pp. 108–11.

Evangelical Alliance. 2006. *Faith and Nation* (www.eauk.org).

Favell, Adrian. 1997. *Philosophies of Integration*. London: Macmillan.

Ferrari, Silvio. 1995. 'The emergent pattern of church and state in western Europe'. *Brigham Young University Law Review*, 421–37.

Ferry, Jules. 1883. *Lettre aux instituteurs*. Available at: http://s.huet.free.fr/paideia/paidogonos/jferry3.htm (last accessed 5 March 2006).

Fetzer, Joel and Christopher Soper. 2005. *Muslims and the State in Britain, France, and Germany*. New York: Cambridge University Press.

Foner, Nancy and Richard Alba. 2007. *Immigrant Religion in the US and Western Europe*. Typescript.

Fukuyama, Francis. 2006. 'Identity, immigration, and liberal democracy'. *Journal of Democracy*, 17 (2), 5–20.

Gaspard, Françoise and Farhad Khosrokhavar. 1995. *Le Foulard et la république*. Paris: La Découverte.

Gauchet, Marcel. 1997. *The Disenchantment of the World*. Princeton, NJ: Princeton University Press.

Gellner, Ernest. 1981. *Muslim Society*. Cambridge: Cambridge University Press.

Gellner, Ernest. 1992. *Postmodernism, Reason and Religion*. London: Routledge.

Giry, Stéphanie. 2006. 'France and its Muslims'. *Foreign Affairs*, 85 (5), 87–104.

Glazer, Nathan. 1997. *We Are All Multiculturalists Now*. Cambridge, MA: Harvard University Press.

Göle, Nilüfer. 1996. *The Forbidden Modern*. Ann Arbor: The University of Michigan Press.

Göle, Nilüfer. 2003. 'The voluntary adoption of Islamic stigma symbols'. *Social Research*, n. 2, 809–29.

Goerlich, Helmut. 1999. 'Distanz und Neutralität im Lehrberuf'. *Neue Juristische Wochenschrift*, n. 40, 2929–33.

Gray, John. 2000. *The Two Faces of Liberalism*. Cambridge: Polity Press.

Gresh, Alain. J. 2004. *L'Islam, la république et le monde*. Paris: Fayard.

Gusy, Christoph. 2006. 'Integration und religion: Grundgesetz und Islam'. In Ulrike Davy and Albrecht Weber (eds), *Paradigmenwechsel in Einwanderungsfragen?* Baden-Baden: Nomos.

Habermas, Jürgen. 2006. 'Religion in the public sphere'. *European Journal of Philosophy*, 14 (1), 1–25.

Haddad, Yvonne Yazbeck and Tyler Golson. 2007. 'Overhauling Islam'. *Journal of Church and State*, 49 (3), 487ff.

Hansen, Randall. 2007. 'Free economy and the Jacobin state'. In Carol M. Swain (ed.), *Debating Immigration*, New York: Cambridge University Press.

Haut Conseil à l'intégration. 2000. *L'Islam dans la république*. Paris.

Hayek, Friedrich. 1960. *The Constitution of Liberty*. Chicago: University of Chicago Press.

Heath, Anthony and Soojin Yu. 2005. *Explaining Ethnic Minority Disadvantage* (typescript).

Hepple, Bob and Tufyal Choudhury. 2001. *Tackling Religious Discrimination*. Home Office Research Study 221, Home Office Research, Development and Statistics Directorate, London.

Heinig, Hans Michael and Martin Morlok. 2003. 'Von Schafen und Kopftüchern'. *Juristenzeitung*, 15/16, 777–85.

Higonnet, Patrice. 1988. *Sister Republics*. Cambridge, MA: Harvard University Press.

Hillgruber, Christian. 1999. 'Der deutsche Kulturstaat und der muslimische Kulturimport'. *Juristenzeitung*, 11, 538–47.

Hillgruber, Christian. 2001. 'Der Körperschaftsstatus von Religionsgemeinschaften'. *Neue Zeitschrift für Verwaltungsrecht*, 20 (12), 1347–55.

Huntington, Samuel. 1996. *The Clash of Civilizations and the Remaking of World Order*. New York: Simon and Schuster.

Informationszentrum Asyl und Migration. 2004. *Kopftuchdebatte: Information*. Nürnberg: Bundesamt für die Anerkennung ausländischer Flüchtlinge.

International Crisis Group. 2005. *Understanding Islamism*. Middle East/North Africa Report N. 37, 2 March.

International Crisis Group. 2006. *La France face à ses musulmans*. Rapport Europe N 172, 9 March.

International Crisis Group. 2007. *Islam and Identity in Germany*. Europe Report N. 181, 14 March.

Joppke, Christian. 1999. *Immigration and the Nation–State*. Oxford: Oxford University Press.

Joppke, Christian. 2004. 'The retreat of multiculturalism in the liberal state'. *British Journal of Sociology*, 55 (2), 237–57.

Joppke, Christian. 2005. *Selecting by Origin: Ethnic Migration in the Liberal State*. Cambridge: Harvard University Press.

Joppke, Christian. 2007a. 'State neutrality and Islamic headscarf laws in France and Germany'. *Theory and Society*, vol. 36, 313–42.

Joppke, Christian. 2007b. 'Beyond national models: Civic integration policies for immigrants in western Europe'. *West European Politics*, 30 (1), 2007, 1–22.

Joppke, Christian. 2008. 'Immigration and the identity of citizenship'. *Citizenship Studies* (December issue).

Joppke, Christian. 2009. 'Limits of integration policy: Britain and her Muslims'. *Journal of Ethnic and Migration Studies* (January issue).

Jouili, Jeanette and Schirin Amir-Moazami. 2006. 'Knowledge, empowerment and religious authority among pious Muslim women in France and Germany'. *The Muslim World*, 96, 617–42.

Kaltenbach, Jeanne-Hélene and Michèle Tribalat. 2002. *La République et l'Islam*. Paris: Gallimard.

Kessler, David. 1993. 'Neutralité de l'enseignement public et liberté d'opinion des élèves'. *Revue française de droit administratif*, 9 (1), 112–19.

Klausen, Jytte. 2005. *The Islamic Challenge*. New York: Oxford University Press.

König, Matthias. 2003. *Staatsbürgerschaft und religiöse Pluralität in post-nationalen Konstellationen*. Doctoral Thesis, University of Marburg, April.

Koopmans, Ruud. 2005. *The Failure of Dutch Multiculturalism in Cross-National Perspective*. Typescript.

The Koran. 2003. (translated by N. J. Dawood). London: Penguin.

Küng, Hans. 2004. *Der Islam*. München and Zürich: Piper.

Kumar, Krishan. 2006. 'English and French national identity'. *Nations and Nationalism*, 12 (3), 413–32.

Kymlicka, Will. 2007. 'Multicultural Odysseys'. *Ethnopolitics* 6 (4), 585–97.

Laborde, Cécile. 2000. 'The concept of the state in British and French political thought'. *Political Studies*, vol. 48, 540–57.

Laborde, Cécile. 2005. 'Secular philosophy and Muslim headscarves in schools'. *The Journal of Political Philosophy*, 13 (3), 305–29.

Laurence, Jonathan and Justin Vaisse. 2006. *Integrating Islam*. Washington, DC: Brookings Institution Press.

Levinson, Meira. 1997. 'Liberalism versus democracy? Schooling private citizens in the public square'. *British Journal of Political Science*, 27, 333–60.

Lewis, Bernard. 1992. *The Crisis of Islam*. New York: Random House.

Lewis, Bernard. 1993. *Islam and the West*. New York: Oxford University Press.

Lewis, Bernard. 2002. *What Went Wrong: Western Impact and Middle Eastern Response*. New York: Oxford University Press.

Lorcerie, Françoise. 2005. 'La Politisation du voile islamique en 2003–2004'. In F. Lorcerie (ed.), *La Politisation du voile*. Paris: Harmattan.

Mahmood, Saba. 2001. 'Feminist theory, embodiment, and the docile agent'. *Cultural Anthropology*, 16 (2), 202–36.

Mahmood, Saba. 2005. *Politics of Piety*. Princeton, NJ: Princeton University Press.

Malik, Kenan. 2005. 'Islamophobia myth'. *Prospect*, 20 January.

Martin, David. 1978. *A General Theory of Secularization*. New York: Harper Colophon.

Marty, Martin. 2001. 'Religious fundamentalism'. In *International Encyclopedia of the Social and Behavioral Sciences* (edited by Paul Baltes and Neil J. Smelser). New York: Elsevier, pp. 13119–23.

Marx, Anthony. 2003. *Faith in Nation: Exclusionary Origins of Nationalism*. New York: Oxford University Press.

McGoldrick, Dominic. 2006. *Human Rights and Religion: The Islamic Headscarf Debate in Europe*. Oxford: Hart.

McLeod, Hugh. 1999. 'Protestantism and British identity, 1815–1945'. In Peter van der Veer and Hartmut Lehmann (eds), *Nation and Religion*, Princeton: Princeton University Press.

Messner, Francis, Pierre-Henri Prélet and Jean-Marie Woehrling (eds), 2003. *Traité de droit français des religions*. Paris: Litec.

Morin, Edgar. 1990. 'Le Trou noir de la laïcité'. *Le Débat*, vol. 74, 38–41.

Morlok, Martin and Julian Krüper. 2003. 'Auf dem Weg zum "forum neutrum"?'. *Neue Juristische Wochenschrift*, n. 14, 1020–1.

Nirumand, Bahman. 2008. 'Mohammed-nicht nur ein Sprachrohr Gottes'. *Neue Zürcher Zeitung*, 22 May 2008, p. 45.

Oestreich, Heide. 2004. *Der Kopftuch-Streit*. Frankfurt am Main: Brandes und Apsel.

Parekh, Bhikhu. 2000. *Rethinking Multiculturalism*. Houndmills, Basingstoke: Macmillan Press.

Parekh, Bhikhu. 2001. *The Future of Multi-Ethnic Britain*. London: Runnymede Trust.

Perry, Susan H. 2006. *Unveiling Politicised Islam: Legal Parameters of the Headscarf Issue in France and in Europe*. MSt dissertation, Kellogg College, Oxford University (manuscript on file with author).

Pew Research Center. 2006. *The Great Divide: How Westerners and Muslims View Each Other*. Washington, DC (www.pewglobal.org).

Policy Exchange. 2007. *Living Apart Together: British Muslims and the Paradox of Multiculturalism* (by Munira Mirza, Abi Senthilkumaran and Zein Ja'far). London: Policy Exchange.

'Preventing Extremism Together' Working Groups. August–October 2005. (www.communities.gov.uk/index.asp?id=1502010).

Poole, Thomas. 2005. 'Of headscarves and heresies'. *Public Law* (Winter), 685–95.

Poulter, Sebastian. 1997. 'Muslim headscarves in school'. *Oxford Journal of Legal Studies*, 17 (1), 43–74.

Rawls, John. 1971. *A Theory of Justice*. Cambridge, MA: Harvard University Press.

Rawls, John. 1993. *Political Liberalism*. New York: Columbia University Press.

Rivero, Jean. 1960. 'De l'idéologie à la règle de droit: La Notion de laïcité dans la jurisprudence administrative'. In Centre de sciences politiques de l'institut d'études juridiques de Nice (ed.), *La Laïcité*, Paris: PUF.

Roy, Olivier. 2004. *Globalized Islam*. New York: Columbia University Press.

Roy, Olivier. 2005. *La Laïcité face à l'islam*. Paris: Hachette (translated, by George Jr. Holoch, as *Secularism Confronts Islam*, New York: Columbia University Press, 2007; all references in the text are to the French original).

Ruthven, Malise. 2007. 'How to understand Islam'. *New York Review of Books*, 54 (17), 8 November.

Sackofsky, Ute. 2003. 'Die Kopftuch-Entscheidung'. *Neue Juristische Wochenschrift*, 56 (46), 3298–301.

Sahlins, Peter. 1989. *Boundaries: The Making of France and Spain in the Pyrenees*. Berkeley: University of California Press.

Schain, Martin. 2007. *Multiculturalism and its Discontents*. Typescript.

Scanlon, Thomas. 2003. *The Difficulty of Tolerance*. New York: Cambridge University Press.

Schiffauer, Werner. 2003. 'Muslimische Organisationen und ihr Anspruch auf Repräsentativität'. In Alexandre Esudier (ed.), *Der Islam in Europe*, Göttingen: Wallstein.

Schiek, Dagmar. 2004. 'Just a piece of cloth?'. *The Industrial Law Journal*, 33 (1), 68–73.

Schluchter, Wolfgang. 1991. *Religion und Lebensführung*, vol. 2. Frankfurt am Main: Suhrkamp.

Schnapper, Dominique. 1994. *La Communauté des citoyens*. Paris: Gallimard.

Schnapper, Dominique. 2006. *Providential Democracy*. New Brunswick: Transaction Publishers.

Scott, Joan Wallach. 2005. 'Symptomatic politics'. *French Politics, Culture and Society*, 23 (3), 106–27.

Scott, Joan Wallach. 2007. *The Politics of the Veil*. Princeton, NJ: Princeton University Press.

Sen, Amartya. 2006. 'The uses and abuses of multiculturalism'. *The New Republic*, February 9.

Shadid, W. and P. S. Van Koningsveld. 2005. 'Muslim dress in Europe'. *Journal of Islamic Studies*, vol. 16, 35–61.

Shavit, Uriya. 2007. 'Should Muslims integrate into the West?'. *Middle East Quarterly*, 14 (4), 13–21.

Shils, Edward. 1972. 'Center and periphery'. In E. Shils, *The Constitution of Society*. Chicago: University of Chicago Press.

Simmel, Georg. 1971. 'Group expansion and the development of individuality'. In Donald Levine (ed.), *Georg Simmel: On Individuality and Social Forms*. Chicago: University of Chicago Press.

Skerry, Peter. 2006. 'The American exception'. *Time*, 21 August, p. 30.

Stasi Report. 2003. *Rapport au Président de la République*. Paris: Commission de réflexion sur l'application du principe de laïcité dans la république.

Stolzenberg, Nomi Maya. 1993. ' "He drew a circle that shut me out": Assimilation, indoctrination, and the paradox of liberal education'. *Harvard Law Review*, 106, 581–667.

Stone Sweet, Alec. 2000. *Governing with Judges: Constitutional Politics in Europe*. Oxford: Oxford University Press.

Strayer, Joseph. 1970. *On the Medieval Origins of the Modern State*. Princeton: Princeton University Press.

Thüsing, Gregor and Donat Wege. 2004. 'Das Kopftuch der Muslima vor deutschen und vor britischen Gerichten'. *Zeitschrift für Europäisches Privatrecht*, vol. 12, 399–423.

Tietze, Nikola. 2001. *Islamische Identitäten*. Hamburg: Hamburger Edition.

Tribalat, Michèle. 1995. *Faire France*. Paris: La Découverte.

Venel, Nancy. 1999. *Musulmanes françaises*. Paris: L'Harmattant.

Walter, Christian. 2005. 'Die Rahmenbedingungen für die Kooperation von religiösen Vereinigungen und Staat unter dem Grundgesetz'. In Beauftragte der Bundesregierung für Migration, Flüchtlinge und Integration, *Islam einbürgern*. Bonn: Bonner Universitäts-Buchdruckerei.

Weber, Eugene. 1976. *Peasants into Frenchmen*. Stanford, CA: Stanford University Press.

Weber, Max. 1976. *Wirtschaft und Gesellschaft*. Tübingen: Mohr.

Weber, Max. 1977. *Politik als Beruf*. Tübingen: Mohr.

Weibel, Nadine. 2000. *Par-delà le voile*. Paris: Ed. Complexes.

Weil, Patrick. 2004. 'Lifting the veil of ignorance'. *Progressive Politics*, vol. 3, 1 March, non-paginated.

Willaime, Jean-Paul. 1998. 'Ecole et religions: Une nouvelle donne?'. *Revue Française de Pédagogie*, no 125, 7–20.

William, Jean-Claude. 1991. 'Le Conseil d'Etat et la laïcité'. *Revue française de sciences politiques*, 28–44.

Woehrling, Jean-Marie. 1998. 'Réflexions sur le principe de la neutralité de l'état en matière religieuse et sa mise en œuvre en droit français'. *Archives de Sciences sociales des Religions*, no. 101, 31–52.

Winkler, Heinrich-August. 2007. 'Der Westen braucht den Streit'. *Kölner Stadt-Anzeiger*, 16 February 2007.

Yurdakul, Gökçe and Y. Michal Bodemann. 2006. ' "We don't want to be the Jews of tomorrow" '. *German Politics and Society*, 24 (2), 44–67.

Zolberg, Aristide and Long Litt Woon. 1999. 'Why Islam is like Spanish'. *Politics and Society*, 27 (1), 5–38.

Index

151